Table of Con

About the Authors

 *Frances Wallace*, MPH, is a founding member and former associate director of the National Implementation Research Institute at Louis de la Parte Florida Mental Health Institute, at the University of South Florida. Frances obtained her Bachelor of Science degree in Family, Child, and Consumer Science from Florida State University and a Master of Public Health degree from the University of South Florida, with a focus on maternal and child health. Her current research interests include implementation of evidence-based programs, systems of care for children's mental health, and systems methodologies applied to organizational and system transformation efforts. Her recent work includes investigating the factors that influence the success of attempted implementations of evidence-based practices and programs in systems of care, evaluating state behavioral health systems for children, and provision of implementation technical assistance.

 **Karen A. Blase,** Ph.D., has been a program developer, researcher, trainer, program evaluator, and published author in the human service field for over 30 years. Karen received her doctorate in Developmental and Child Psychology from the University of Kansas, with a focus on school-based interventions, child welfare, and community-based services for children and youth involved with juvenile justice. Her professional career has involved research and technical assistance focused on replicating evidence-based programs and practices, as well as developing collaborative service networks to address important social issues in the U.S. and in Canada (e.g., domestic violence, juvenile justice, child welfare).

A major interest has been the development, implementation, adaptation, and quality improvement of exemplary service models, evidence-based programs and practices, and strategies for effective scale-up and systems change. As part of a research team, Dr. Blase was involved in completing a major review and synthesis of the implementation literature (http://nirn.fmhi.usf.edu/resources/publications/Monograph/index.cfm). This extensive review of implementation strategies and proposed frameworks is providing guidance for the adoption and utilization of evidence-based programs and practices. Karen formerly was a research professor at the Louis de la Parte Florida Mental Health Institute, at the University of South Florida, and is co-director of the National Implementation Research Network (http://nirn.fmhi.usf.edu), formerly at the Louis de la Parte Florida Mental Health Institute and now at the Frank Porter Graham Child Development Institute at the University of North Carolina at Chapel Hill. She is also a co-director of the OSEP TA Center for State Implementation and Scaling-Up of Evidence-Based Practices (www.scalingup.org). Karen is currently a senior scientist at the Frank Porter Graham Child Development Institute at the University of North Carolina at Chapel Hill. She may be reached at kblase@mail.fpg.unc.edu.

***Dean Fixsen,*** Ph.D., began his career in human services in 1963 as a psychiatric aide in a large state hospital for children with profound developmental delays. Dean received his doctorate in Experimental Psychology from the University of Kansas in 1970. He has spent his career developing and implementing evidence-based programs, initiating and managing change processes in provider organizations and service delivery systems, and working with others to improve the lives of children, families, and adults. Over the past five decades, Dean has co-authored nearly 100 publications, including the highly regarded monograph, *Implementation Research: A Synthesis of the Literature* (http://nirn.fmhi.usf.edu/resources/ publications/Monograph/index.cfm). He has served on numerous editorial boards (including *Implementation Science;* http://www.implementationscience.com/) and has advised local, state, and federal governments. Dean formerly was a research professor at the Louis de la Parte Florida Mental Health Institute, and is co-director of the National Implementation Research Network (http://nirn.fmhi. usf.edu) and the State Implementation and Scaling-Up of Evidence-Based Practices (SISEP) Center (www.scalingup.org). Dean is currently a senior scientist at the Frank Porter Graham Child Development Institute at the University of North Carolina at Chapel Hill. He may be reached at dfixsen@mail.fpg.unc.edu.

Sandra Naoom, MSPH, is an associate director and founding member of the National Implementation Research Network at the Louis de la Parte Florida Mental Health Institute, University of South Florida. Sandra obtained her B.A. in Psychology from George Washington University and her Masters of Science in Public Health, with a concentration in Behavioral Health, from the University of South Florida. Sandra is currently obtaining her Ph.D. in Measurement and Evaluation from the USF College of Education. Sandra's current research interests are related to dissemination and implementation of evidence-based programs and practices, the development of fidelity instruments, and the development of instruments to assess implementation. Sandra has over 9 years of research experience. Her recent efforts include the synthesis of the implementation literature, a qualitative research study exploring the capacity and perceived responsibility of evidence-based program developers as they help others adopt and implement their program/ practice, the design and analyses of school-based implementation studies of prevention programs, the development of instruments to assess fidelity and implementation, and consultation, evaluation, and technical assistance related to implementation of innovations with fidelity.

Foreword

District and school administrators at every level want to use the findings of good, up-to-date research to improve outcomes for their students. The use of scientifically based instruction was a priority long before the fairly recent federal requirements in this area.

However, efforts to bring the findings of research into the classroom in a meaningful way are often frustrated by the knowledge needed to understand the research and to understand what is involved in implementing research-based practices successfully. The knowledge and skills involved in understanding and evaluating research and an in-depth understanding of the implementation process are equally critical in bridging the gap—too often a chasm—between research and practice. The bridge first involves learning about and selecting a program or practice, which calls for skill in understanding and evaluating research. The second step concerns "fidelity of implementation." This step—all too often the missing link—spells the difference between success and failure, as the practice or program must be implemented in the way the developer intended if it is to achieve the success demonstrated by the research.

This important volume addresses the implementation of research findings in the schools in a way that sheds new light on the subject. The authors present and clarify the essential components and stages of the implementation process, which frequently have not been addressed with the practitioners most in need of the information. And the authors provide guidance to school personnel in how to achieve fidelity of implementation.

As additional resources, we have appended to the book three articles on understanding and evaluating research, two published online by the Institute of Education Sciences in the U.S. Department of Education, and one published in *Exceptional Children*, the research journal of the Council for Exceptional Children.

Educational Research Service is proud to publish the work of Frances Wallace, Karen Blase, Dean Fixsen, and Sandra Naoom of the National Implementation Research Institute. Our goal at ERS is to bring you the research knowledge you need to improve the education of everyone's children, and we hope this book helps you to meet your goals.

Kathleen McLane
Chief Knowledge Officer
Educational Research Service

Foreword

Acknowledgements

ERS wishes to express its gratitude and appreciation to Mr. and Mrs. Roy Wilson for supporting the production and marketing of this book through a special contribution, made to honor Dr. Glen Robinson. The Wilsons wish to acknowledge Dr. Robinson for his years of service as the first President of ERS. From 1973-1994, Dr. Robinson worked to provide educators with the best research-based materials to help improve the education of our children and youth.

Dr. Robinson is a strong believer in the use of research in educational decision making, and in the role of ERS in assisting school districts to use research to improve our schools. While Mr. Wilson served as the executive director of the National School Public Relations Association (NSPRA), Dr. Robinson worked with him and three other board members to establish ERS as an independent nonprofit research organization to serve the research and information needs of educators across the country.

It is particularly appropriate that the Wilsons' gift be used for the dissemination of this book. The work of Frances Wallace, Karen Blase, Dean Fixsen, and Sandra Naoom presented in this publication explores what is involved in the effective implementation of research-based programs and practices, which is at the heart of what we strive to do at ERS. We thank Mr. and Mrs. Wilson for helping to bring this publication to the educational leaders who need it, and we look forward to continuing the tradition that Dr. Robinson began in 1973.

Chapter 1

Introduction: Using Research to Improve Practice

Do you want to make use of the latest research-based findings in order to improve student achievement, reduce student behavior problems, or improve relationships with parents and community members? Would you like to:

- improve student academic achievement significantly (e.g., Direct Instruction: Becker & Engelmann, 1995; Success for All: Slavin & Madden,1999)?
- reduce referrals to special education by over 50% (e.g., Project ACHIEVE: Knoff, 2005)?
- reduce office discipline referrals by over 50% (e.g., schoolwide Positive Behavior Support: Sugai & Horner, 2002)?
- improve reading achievement (e.g., Success for All: Slavin & Madden, 2006)?
- reduce high school dropout rates by 50% (e.g., STEP program: Felner et al., 2001)?
- reduce the incidence of childhood depression by over 50% (e.g., Kam, Greenberg & Kusché, 2004)?

Do you want to see other education research put to use to benefit the students in your schools? If so, you are interested in the science and practice of implementation, the subject of this book.

Currently, it is difficult for leaders in practice settings such as schools to make use of the products of science. This has been referred to as the "science-to-service gap" and the "quality chasm." As noted above, research has demonstrated the benefits of doing things in new ways that clearly provide very desirable results to students, schools, and communities. For several decades, funding agencies, researchers, scholars, and practitioners have been frustrated with the apparent inability of schools and other service settings to make use of those research-based methods. The good news is that people have not stopped trying. Out of their efforts and the evaluation of their efforts, new methods are emerging to more reliably and effectively bridge the science-to-service gap. These new methods are forming the foundation for the practice and science of implementation.

In its simplest form, implementation is a multiplication problem:

Innovation x Teacher x School x Educational Policies x Purveyor = Student and School Outcomes

Like any math problem, if all the factors are 1.0, the outcome is 1.0. Similarly, if any one of the factors is zero, the outcome is zero. In addition, the formula tells us that the product can never exceed the smallest factor in the formula (if all but one of the factors is 1.0 and the exception is 0.25, the product will be 0.25). Thus, each factor in this equation is critical to the success of any implementation effort.

What are the factors in this formula for success? For our purposes, they are:

- Innovation–The educational innovation must be clearly described and operationalized so that it can be taught, learned, and used to produce the intended results.
- Teacher–The teacher must be well-prepared, supported, and motivated to use the innovation.
- School–The administration must provide leadership and be able to change school structures and functions so that teachers can learn and use the innovation effectively.
- Educational Policies–District and state policies need to be modified and aligned to support the schools' and teachers' effective use of the innovation.
- Purveyor–A purveyor (i.e., a group of individuals representing a program or practice) needs to be available to actively work with the school to implement the educational innovation with fidelity and good effect.
- Student and School Outcomes–The various academic, social, and community benefits that are the goals of quality education.

Literature and Practice Reviews

In this book, we will focus on the conceptual and practical knowledge principals, superintendents, and education board members need to make full and effective use of evidence-based education innovations. The findings described in this book are the result of an intensive review of implementation evaluation literature and a review of successful implementation practices carried out by purveyors across the nation. The literature review includes reports of any efforts to collect data or attempts to implement practices or programs in any domain (including agriculture, business, child welfare, education, engineering, health, juvenile justice, manufacturing, medicine, mental health, nursing, social services, and substance abuse). Nearly 2,000 citations were found, 1,054 met the criteria for inclusion in the review, and 743 remained after a full text review. The full results of the literature review have been reported in a monograph (Fixsen, Naoom, Blase, Friedman, & Wallace, 2005). An interesting finding from this extensive review of the literature is that the best evidence points to what does *not* work with respect to implementation. The results of several carefully designed studies confirm two conclusions (also see similar conclusions reached in reviews by Ellis et al., 2003, and Greenhalgh, Robert, MacFarlane, Bate, & Kyriakidou, 2004):

- Information dissemination alone (research literature, mailings, promulgation of practice guidelines) is an ineffective implementation method.

- Training alone (no matter how well done) is an ineffective implementation method.

Although these have been two of the most widely used methods for attempting implementation of policies, programs, and practices, they repeatedly have been shown to be ineffective in education, human services, health, business, and manufacturing. This finding has clear implications for policy makers, state planners, education leaders, and purveyors. A different approach needs to be taken to implement policies, programs, and practices effectively.

The implementation practice review included a series of meetings of those who are actively involved as purveyors, implementers, policy makers, and researchers related to specific research-based approaches to solving problems in education and other human services. We used concept mapping and modified nominal group procedures to collect information systematically in these meetings. A complete report of the analysis of the practice reviews can be found on the National Implementation Research Network Web site (http://nirn. fmhi.usf.edu). We also draw upon the broader literature on implementation as we focus on issues more specific to education in this book. It was interesting to see how well the results from the practice review fit with the results from the literature review. The frameworks for successful implementation presented in this book are well founded in the literature and current best practices, and provide a point of departure for future development of the science and practice of implementation.

In this book, we outline the differences between interventions and implementation, then move on to define the core components of interventions and the importance of ensuring the full application of those core components during the implementation process. Next, we overview the kinds of implementation outcomes we identified in the literature and their relationship to outcomes for students. This is followed by a description of the key role that program purveyors have in achieving successful implementation outcomes. With these concepts as a foundation, we then describe the stages of implementation and "implementation drivers," the most important parts of this book. There is no doubt that successful implementation requires careful planning, hard work, and persistence over several years. There also is no doubt that the benefits of effectively implementing research-based innovations in schools far outweigh the costs.

An Implementation Headset

To fully understand this book, the reader needs to adopt an implementation point of view. From an implementation point of view, there are always two important aspects of every research study, demonstration project, or attempted use of an innovation. In each instance, there are *intervention* processes and outcomes and there are *implementation* processes and outcomes. When implementing evidence-based practices and programs, Blase, Fixsen, and Phillips (1984) discussed the need to discriminate implementation outcomes (Are they doing the program as intended?) from intervention outcomes (Yes, they are, and it is/is not resulting in good outcomes.). Only when effective innovations are fully implemented should we expect positive outcomes (Bernfeld, 2001; Fixsen & Blase, 1993; Institute of Medicine—Committee on Quality of Health Care in America, 2001; Washington State Institute for Public Policy, 2002).

As we conducted the reviews, we noticed that the activities involved in creating educational innovations and the activities involved in implementing those innovations are very different. Innovations are developed and validated through well-designed research. One innovation can be the product of limited research and another might be the subject of dozens of studies. When it came to implementing those innovations to achieve improved outcomes, the amount of research on the effectiveness of the innovation did not matter. What mattered was the effectiveness of the activities involved in implementing those innovations. For example, the effectiveness of the Success for All (SFA) education program is supported by over 40 well-designed research studies (Slavin, Madden, & Datnow, 2005). The usefulness

Table 1.1. Relationship Between Implementation and Innovation			
		Implementation	
		Effective	Not Effective
Innovation	Effective	**Improved Outcomes**	Poor Outcomes
	Not Effective	Poor Outcomes	Poor Outcomes

of the SFA program in nearly 2,000 schools is supported by well-designed implementation strategies carried out by a well-organized purveyor group (the Success for All Foundation). Thus, an innovation is one thing, the implementation of an innovation is another thing altogether. As shown in Table 1.1, improved outcomes in education are the product of effective innovations *and* effective implementation efforts. Effective innovations that are not implemented effectively result in poor educational outcomes. Similarly, effective implementation of ineffective innovations results in poor educational outcomes.

Conclusion: Education leaders need to pay attention to: 1) the research basis for an innovation, and 2) the strategies needed to implement that innovation in order to achieve improved educational outcomes. An intervention must be well defined and carefully evaluated with regard to its effects on its intended consumers (students, families, adults). Likewise, implementation of an intervention must be well defined and carefully evaluated with regard to its effects on its intended consumers (teachers, administrators, schools, and systems).

Core Components Defined

The next concept that needs to be understood is the idea of "core components." We have adopted this phrase to reflect the knowledge base that exists in "information economics" (see Winter & Szulanski, 2001), a division of economics first developed by Nobel prize winner Kenneth Arrow. Unlike other economic goods, information is enhanced with use, not depleted, thus engendering a new division of economics. The core components specify "which traits are replicable, how these attributes are created, and the characteristics of environments in which they are worth replicating" (Winter & Szulanski, 2001, p. 733). Thus, core components refer to the most essential and indispensable components of an *intervention* practice or program ("core intervention components"), or the most essential and indispensable components of an *implementation* practice or program ("core implementation components").

Core Intervention Components

There is some evidence that the more clearly the core components of an intervention program or practice are known and defined, the more readily the innovation can be implemented successfully (Bauman, Stein, & Ireys, 1991; Dale, Baker, & Racine, 2002; Fashola & Slavin, 1997; Winter & Szulanski, 2001). From an implementation point of view, the particular innovation being implemented could be anything: methods to more effectively teach reading, writing, and mathematics; pull-out or whole-school innovations; new instructional strategies; comprehensive school reform programs; or school management programs.

The New American Schools Development Corporation's demonstration phase evaluation study conducted by Bodilly (1996) sheds light on the importance of identifying and understanding core components. The nine educational programs included in the study represented core, comprehensive, and systemic reform programs. The core programs focused primarily on changing the core reading/writing/mathematics elements of the schools, while the comprehensive programs focused on changing more organizational components along with changes to the core. The one systemic effort took the comprehensive focus one step further by including components that would alter the systems in which the school operated. In addition, the programs ranged from being highly prescriptive to relying on site-based development (i.e., teacher development of either all or part of the program content/curriculum). The study found that those program developers with highly prescriptive components that were clearly communicated were more successful at getting all of the components fully implemented by the end of the demonstration year. Those programs that relied on teacher development of the program were less successful. Overall, the program developers learned that teachers were not interested in developing a new program when they were already consumed with their current responsibilities. Teachers preferred that a highly prescribed program with clearly described core components be presented for implementation. In addition, the developers discovered the need to identify and prioritize components for phased implementation, as opposed to inundating administrators, teachers, and staff with too much too soon.

Conclusion: The speed and effectiveness of implementation may depend upon knowing exactly what has to be in place to achieve the desired results for consumers and stakeholders: no more and no less (Arthur & Blitz, 2000; Fixsen & Blase, 1993; Winter & Szulanski, 2001). Not knowing the core intervention components leads to time and resources wasted on attempting to implement a variety of (if only we knew) nonfunctional elements. Knowing the core intervention components may allow for more efficient and cost-effective implementation and lead to confident decisions about what can be adapted to suit local conditions at an implementation site. Clear descriptions allow for evaluations of the functions of those procedures. Knowing the core intervention components seems essential to answering persistent questions about local adaptations of innovations. Core intervention components are just that; they are essential to achieving the outcomes desired for students, schools, and communities.

Chapter 2
Adopt, Adapt, or Implement?

A large and varied literature exists describing "diffusion" of information and how individuals and organizations make "adoption decisions" (Fitzgerald, Ferlie, & Hawkins, 2003; Rogers, 1983; Westphal, Gulati, & Shortell, 1997). Rogers' work has been influential and is often cited as the conceptual model used by others. For many years, it was thought that "strict implementation" was impossible to achieve, and that local adaptations were inevitable (Rogers, 1983) if "diffusion" of innovations occurred on a national scale. However, deciding to adopt an educational innovation should not be confused with actually putting that program or practice into effective use. Rogers (1983) observed that fewer than 3% of the more than 1,000 articles he reviewed pertained to implementation. He noted that the diffusion literature takes us up to the point of deciding to adopt an innovation and says nothing about what to do next to implement that innovation with fidelity. This sentiment is reiterated in Cooper, Slavin, and Madden's (1998) research regarding teachers' use of a community of practice on building activities, where they concluded that "Our qualitative data suggests that a yes vote for adoption does not always translate into a yes vote for implementation" (p. 405).

In the past 20 years, evaluations have demonstrated that it is possible to implement innovations on a large scale with a high degree of fidelity (e.g., Bodilly, 1996; Elliott & Mihalic, 2004; Fagan & Mihalic, 2003; Fixsen, Blase, Timbers, & Wolf, 2001; Gill et al., 2005; Kirby, Berends, & Naftel, 2001; Mihalic & Irwin, 2003; Schoenwald, Sheidow, & Letourneau, 2004; Schoenwald, Sheidow, Letourneau, & Liao, 2003; Slavin & Madden, 1999). Adaptation no longer is seen as a necessary and desirable part of implementation efforts. Thus, the question becomes, "What must be maintained in order to achieve fidelity and effectiveness at the student level?" The answer is: core intervention components that have been demonstrated to account for positive changes for students must be implemented. The core intervention components are, by definition, essential to achieving good outcomes for students and others at an implementation site. However, understanding and adhering to the principles of intervention underlying each core component may (within limits) allow for flexibility in *form* (e.g., processes and strategies) without sacrificing the *function* associated with the component. For example, Bierman et al. (2002) of the Conduct Prevention Research Group noted in their analysis of large-scale implementation of the school- and community-based Fast Track Program that:

> To maintain the fidelity of the prevention program, it was important to maintain a central focus on the protective and risk factors identified in developmental research, and to employ intervention strategies that had proven effective in previous clinical trials. Yet, at the same time, flexibility was needed to adapt the intervention in order to engage heterogeneous participants who represented a range of demographic characteristics and cultural backgrounds (pp. 9-10).

In practical terms this meant that acceptable menus for skill presentations and a variety of practice activities were offered to allow Fast Track Program group leaders to tailor sessions (within limits) to the interests of the children.

Thus, the specification of core intervention components is very important to the process of developing evidence-based practices and programs, preparing programs for large-scale implementation, and monitoring the use of core components in practice to ensure that underlying concepts and goals are adhered to over time and across schools. The function of core components must be maintained if the demonstrated outcomes of an innovation are to be realized at each school. Adaptations that vary the form of the innovation's components are acceptable, provided those adaptations preserve the function and do not diminish the demonstrated benefits of the innovation.

Conclusion: Knowing the core components of intervention programs and practices and their underlying principles is important to successful implementation efforts. Detailed descriptions are helpful and a good place to begin, but the eventual specification of the core intervention components for any program or practice may depend upon careful research and well-evaluated experiential learning from a number of attempted replications. Such research and replication efforts may promote an increasingly clear elucidation of the core intervention components and principles, and an understanding of the flexibility and the limits to program modifications.

Degrees of Implementation

What is "implementation?" Implementation is defined as a specified set of activities designed to put into practice an activity or program of known dimensions. Implementation is not an event. It is a mission-oriented process involving multiple decisions, well-organized actions, and real-time corrections. Various authors have discussed the outcomes of implementation attempts in different ways (Goggin, 1986). The outcomes of implementation might be categorized as follows:

Paper implementation means putting into place new policies and procedures, with the adoption of an innovation as the rationale for the policies and procedures. The problem is, implementation often stops there. One estimate is that 80-90% of the person-to-person innovations in business stop at paper implementation (Rogers, 2002). Westphal et al. (1997) found in their survey of businesses that, "If organizations can minimize evaluation and inspection of their internal operations by external constituents through adoption alone, they may neglect implementation altogether, decoupling operational routines from formally adopted programs" (p. 371). A similar result was found in a careful study of implementation of new sun protection/skin cancer prevention practices in Australia. Nearly all of the primary or secondary schools adopted the recommended comprehensive sun protection policy, but only a few actually implemented the recommended sun protection practices (Schofield, Edwards, & Pearce, 1997). Thus, paper implementation may be especially prevalent when outside groups are monitoring compliance (e.g., for accreditation) and much of the monitoring focuses on the paper trail. It is clear that paperwork in file cabinets plus manuals on shelves do not equal putting innovations into practice with benefits to consumers.

Process implementation means putting new operating procedures in place to conduct training workshops, provide supervision, change information reporting forms, and so on, with the adoption of an innovation as the rationale for the procedures. The activities related to an innovation are occurring, events are being counted, and innovation-related language is adopted. The problem is that not much of what goes on is functionally related to the new practice. Training (such as professional development days for teachers) might consist of merely didactic orientation to the new practice or program, supervision might be unrelated to and uninformed by what was taught in training, information might be collected and stored without affecting decision making, and the terms used in the new innovation-related language may be devoid of operational meaning and impact. In business, this form of implementation has been called the Fallacy of Programmatic Change. That is, the belief that promulgating organizational mission statements, "corporate culture" programs, training courses, or quality circles will transform organizations, and that employee behavior is changed simply by altering a company's formal structure and systems (Beer, Eisenstat, & Spector, 1990). It is clear that the trappings of evidence-based practices and programs plus lip service do not equal putting innovations into practice with benefits to students, schools, and communities.

Performance implementation means putting innovations in place in such a way that the identified core intervention components are used with good effect for consumers (Paine, Bellamy, & Wilcox, 1984).

It appears that implementation that produces actual benefits to students, schools, and communities requires more careful and thoughtful efforts, as outlined in this book.

Chapter 3
Purveyors

How can performance implementation be achieved routinely in the real world of education? Our reviews indicate that, "Effective programs are disseminated by organizations that focus on the quality of implementation" (Fashola & Slavin, 1997). Thus, it is important to understand the idea and role of a "purveyor." A purveyor is a group of individuals representing a program or practice who actively work to implement that practice or program with fidelity and good effect. For example, the Success for All Foundation is the purveyor of the Success for All (SFA) school program. MST Services, Inc. is the purveyor of the Multisystemic Treatment program for children in the delinquency system. These are clear-cut examples of purveyors, and each has a set of activities designed to help new schools or other organizations ("implementation sites") implement their respective programs. Over the years, a purveyor also has been described as a "change agent" (Fairweather, Sanders, & Tornatzy, 1974; Havelock & Havelock, 1973), "site coordinator" (Blase et al., 1984), "design-based assistance organization" (Bodilly, 1996), "program consultant" (Gendreau, Goggin, & Smith, 1999), "linking agent" (Kraft, Mezoff, Sogolow, Neumann, & Thomas, 2000), and "site facilitator" (Datnow & Castellano, 2000).

Rohrbach, D'Onofrio, Backer, and Montgomery (1996) identified the importance of purveyors to many aspects of the implementation process in education settings. Purveyors with direct knowledge

about the innovation are in personal contact with teachers, administrators, and other relevant school personnel to allow a free exchange
of information. Purveyors and school personnel work as a team to
diagnose any problems that may impede program implementation
and develop action plans to address them. Purveyors act as outside
consultants or change agents to provide objectivity about which innovation provides the best fit and what needs to be done to get the
innovations implemented. Purveyors help to identify the core innovation components and identify the elements that may be rein-
vented by teachers. Purveyors help to inform and generate enthusiasm for innovations and encourage personnel to take leadership
roles in getting them implemented. Purveyors help design strategies
to identify and recruit specific teachers to become program champions at their schools, and recruit teachers who have mastered implementation to help train and coach other teachers. Purveyors help
teachers and key administrators as they struggle with decisions about
program implementation.

Bodilly's (1996) work on the New American Schools (NAS) Demonstration Project provides additional insight into the activities and expectations of a purveyor group. Through the NAS three-phase project,
educational programs were designed (both core and comprehensive)
and the potential for scale-up was studied, in part through the examination of implementation and site development strategies utilized by
design teams at the school level. The study of these strategies across
the programs allowed the researchers to pinpoint effective strategies
and roll these into a set of generalized attributes needed by potential purveyors to implement programs across sites. These attributes
include (1) well-defined leadership at the program developer level;
(2) purveyor staff that are dedicated to the program and understand

the program inside and out (developed by the program itself or by contracted staff); (3) a well-developed implementation plan and goals clearly communicated to all engaged in the implementation of the program; (4) feedback mechanisms at the implementation site level that allow for critical self-analysis and motivation toward goals and improvement; (5) a set of implementation strategies that allow for site selection assessments, relationship development with sites, provision of ongoing flow of information to the site (training, materials), infrastructure support, assessment of fidelity, and feedback; and (6) the use of demonstration sites for purveyors to improve their programs through experience and knowledge accumulation over time, to provide a model for new sites, and add credibility to the program.

An advantage of having a well-organized and persistent approach to implementation of innovations may be that the purveyor can accumulate knowledge over time (Fixsen & Blase, 1993; Fixsen, Phillips, & Wolf, 1978; Winter & Szulanski, 2001). Each attempted implementation of the program reveals barriers that need to be overcome and their (eventual) solutions. Problems encountered later on may be preventable with different actions earlier in the implementation process. Thus, with experience, the purveyor groups can learn to change their approaches early in the process in order to avoid some of the later problems. In addition, an experienced purveyor can describe to the managers of an implementation site the likely problems that will arise and the likely solutions that can be applied. This seems to engender confidence and may lead to greater persistence to "see it through" when the going gets rough during the early stages of implementation. The problem is that the feedback loops for implementation efforts are very long. It often takes years to develop an implementation site and then see how well that site performs with respect to implementation and intervention outcomes, and a few more years to adjust strategies and experience new results in an ongoing iterative process (Blase et al., 1984; Fixsen & Blase, 1993; Fixsen et al., 2001). Having a consistent group involved as purveyors of a given program or practice may provide a repository for (more or less carefully evaluated) experiential knowledge and wisdom accumulated from a series of (more or less successful) implementation attempts over many years (Schofield, 2004).

There is a problem, however. At this stage in the development of evidence-based innovations and their implementation, we have learned that many innovations are "orphans" and have no purveyor group connected with the program. Another problem is that not all purveyors are created equal: many developers provide some materials and training and perhaps some telephone advice, but no "service after the sale." Others, unfortunately not many, provide a full range of implementation services to a school and are heavily invested in making sure the students at each school benefit fully from the innovation. If you run into these problems, what can education leaders do? Education leaders can create their own "implementation team" and have it function as a purveyor. An implementation team often consists of a top administrator, a staff person or two, and a teacher or other member of the instructional staff. The important thing is to empower the implementation team to plan and help bring about actual changes in school functions to implement the innovation effectively. This requires leadership to empower the team and follow its recommendations, and it requires freeing up time for the team members to do the hard work of implementation over a period of 2 to 4 years. This strategy has been used successfully in business, but only seems to work when top management fully and consistently supports the work of the team. In any case, in the absence of a real purveyor of an innovation, create an implementation team and charge the team with the responsibilities and duties outlined for purveyors in this book.

Chapter 4
Stages of Implementation

Purveyors are very active during the implementation process. Purveyors work with schools and communities to help them explore the advantages and disadvantages of using an innovation, they provide "service after the sale" by working on-site with administrators and teachers to help them prepare to use the innovation, and purveyors work with teachers, administrators, and policy makers/funders to ensure full implementation and sustainability of the innovation. Our reviews of the literature and successful practices make it clear that implementation does not happen all at once or proceed smoothly, at least not at first. In education, Gill et al. (2005) noted that, "In today's high-stakes accountability environment, district and school staff typically face pressure to demonstrate immediate gains in student achievement. But reforming schools takes time. It is important that everyone involved ... understand[s] that the desired results might not materialize for a few years" (p. xxxiv). Based on their analyses of franchised businesses, Winter and Szulanski (2001) stated that, "We treat knowledge transfer as a process (not a one-time act) by which [a purveyor] recreates a complex, causally ambiguous set of routines in new settings and keeps it functioning. The [purveyor] gradually hones [his or her] ability to manage such a process through experience and repetition" (p. 741). Thus, a purveyor can help organizations and systems stay on track for a few years, and can help recognize and solve common implementation problems in a timely and effective manner (e.g., Blase & Fixsen, 2003; Cheung & Cheng, 1997;

Faggin, 1985; Feldman, Baler, & Penner, 1997; Fox & Gershman, 2000; Rogers, 2002; Williams, 1975; Zins & Illback, 1995).

Our reviews of the implementation literature and implementation practices have led to the identification of six stages of implementation. The stages are:

1. exploration and adoption
2. installation
3. initial implementation
4. full implementation
5. innovation
6. sustainability

Language is linear, so the stages are presented one at a time. However, in practice, the stages are not linear. For example, actions critical to the sustainability stage begin during the exploration stage, and some aspects of an innovation may be in the installation stage while, at the same time, other aspects are in the initial implementation stage. Nevertheless, the stages seem to be useful for those planning and carrying out implementation efforts in education and other human services.

Exploration and Adoption

At some point, someone has to think about making use of an innovation. This requires some degree of awareness of new possibilities that leads to acquisition of information and exploration of options. The purpose of exploration is to assess the potential match between practice and program needs and resources and to make a decision to proceed (or not). The best reason to pursue implementation of an education innovation is to help solve a problem or accomplish a goal with respect to student behavior or achievement. Implementation under these conditions stands a much better chance of success for students, teachers, schools, and communities. The worst reasons to pursue implementation of an innovation are:

- Funding was available and we decided to get our share.
- Government (or the district) has mandated this change and we have to toe the line.
- We want to be seen as progressive, so we adopt many new ideas that come along.

Implementations under these conditions almost never work, and the ones that are successful rarely are sustained (Nutt, 2002). Implementation is too much work and is too disruptive to schools to be done for the wrong reasons.

Considerable attention has been paid to the exploration stage of implementation. Under the best circumstances, the developer of the innovation has created a purveyor group that is skilled at helping education leaders explore the options and make an informed choice. Not every innovation is a good fit with every school or set of issues faced by a school. Purveyors are not interested in wasting their limited resources, nor those of the school, when there is a poor fit between the operational demands/benefits of an innovation and the needs and resources of a school. Purveyors also tend to be well informed about other options available to educators, and can help school leaders find innovations that are a better fit with their needs. Purveyors can provide efficient and effective support to education leaders during the exploration stage. In the absence of a competent purveyor, school leaders are left to their own abilities to obtain reliable information about innovations and carry out the exploration stage using their own staff and resources.

In either case, the exploration stage is very important to the long-term success of the implementation of an innovation. Elias, Zins, Graczyk, and Weissberg (2003) stress that "Long-term dangers accrue when one bypasses the front-end time needed to build constituencies committed to the goals and process of change; to look honestly at the current state of conditions, services, and resources; and establish management capacities…" (p. 309). This is an especially sobering thought when researchers such as Bodilly (1996), Cawelti and Protheroe (2003), and Slavin and Madden (1999) have found that administrators, teachers, districts, and schools are not making good informed choices when choosing programs to adopt and implement. To improve the process, Slavin and Madden have suggested the use of "local brokers" (or purveyors) who would be able to provide administrators and teachers guidance about effective programs, organizational and change processes, and the needs and resources at the local level (p.17).

Han and Weiss (2005) describe the preimplementation phase as the time when teachers and administrators are exposed to the new program, make a decision regarding adoption, and begin implementation planning. The authors stress the importance of several teacher-related or program-related factors during the exploration stage that may influence the implementation process. The authors found that a key factor was the attributes and judgments made by teachers about the program prior to adoption. Teachers' judgments included whether or not the program matched with the needs of the target students, how severe the problems were at the school level (need), the time needed to implement the program, whether or not the program matched the teaching philosophy of the teacher, and the promised intended outcomes offered by the program. In addition, Han and Weiss found that the more knowledgeable the teachers were about the program's core elements, the more likely they were to rate it as an acceptable program. The importance of teacher support is also reflected in the work of Kirby et al. (2001) who examined the 4th year of implementation of seven reform programs. The study found that teacher support of the program led to a higher degree of implementation of the program and also served to reinforce the overall school-level implementation.

Thus, buy-in, commitment, and program acceptance during the exploration stage seem to have a big impact on the success and sustainability of programs in education (Bodilly, 1996; Calweti & Protheroe, 2003; Cooper et al., 1998; Datnow & Castellano, 2000; Denton, Vaughn, & Fletcher, 2003; Fagan & Mihalic, 2003; Fashola & Slavin, 1997; Han & Weiss, 2005; Schaffer, Nesselrodt, & Stringfield, 1997; Slavin & Madden, 1999). In their review of 33 schools' reform, classroom instruction, curriculum-specific, and tutor programs, Fashola and Slavin (1997) found that the "…most successful programs have some buy-in procedure to ensure that participating teachers or whole-school staffs have made an informed and uncoerced choice to use a given program" (p. 10). For example, the SFA and schoolwide Positive Behavior Support (PBS) comprehensive school programs require that teachers and administrators participate in an orientation process, then vote on whether or not to adopt and implement the program (Datnow & Castellano, 2000; Horner & Sugai,

2005; Slavin & Madden, 1999). Through the voting process, 80% of the teachers and administrators must agree to the use of the program in order to have SFA or schoolwide PBS work with the school. SFA and schoolwide PBS achieve buy-in through school awareness processes where all of the teachers and staff are exposed to the core components of the intervention, questions regarding the curriculum and implementation can be answered, and information is provided up front by the purveyor staff on what it will take to implement and sustain the program. Thus, teachers and administrators enter into an agreement and contract with SFA or schoolwide PBS fully aware of what will be taking place at their school and the accountability that is anticipated at the school level. Another school reform effort, the School Development Program (Comer Process) devotes two of their five phases of program implementation to the planning, pre-orientation, and orientation process (Haynes, Emmons, Gebreyesus, & Ben-Avie, 1996). During the planning and preorientation phase, work is done to prepare the district for implementing the program; the orientation phase occurs at the district and school level and includes the dissemination of information about essential elements of the program, goals, and philosophy.

The exploration stage ends when a decision is made to proceed with implementation of an innovation in a given educational setting (Blase et al., 1984; Khatri & Frieden, 2002; Schoenwald & Hoagwood, 2001). It seems clear that innovative practices and programs will not be implemented on any useful scale, nor sustained over the long-term, without the support of political, financial, and education systems at state and local levels (Schoenwald, 1997). That support is garnered during the adoption process and is important throughout all implementation stages.

Conclusion: The exploration stage is a time to assess the needs of students and schools and find out which innovations might match the defined needs. It is also a time to build understanding and enthusiasm for the innovation with the help of the innovation's purveyor. Teacher and stakeholder understanding and buy-in seems to be as important as securing the resources necessary to implement and sustain the innovation.

Program Installation

After a decision is made to begin implementing an education innovation, there are tasks that need to be accomplished before students are exposed to the program or practice. These activities define the installation stage of implementation. Resources are being consumed in active preparation for doing things differently, in keeping with the tenets of the practice or program. Organization change begins when structural supports necessary to initiate the program are put in place. These include ensuring the availability of funding streams, human resource strategies, and policy development, as well as creating reporting frameworks and outcome expectations. Additional resources may be needed to realign current staff, hire new staff members to meet the qualifications required by the program or practice, secure appropriate space, purchase needed technology (e.g., software, computers), fund unreimbursed time in meetings with stakeholders, and fund time for staff while they are in training. These activities and their associated start-up costs are necessary first steps to begin any new human service endeavor.

Experienced purveyors have a clear view of the preparatory steps that need to be taken during the installation stage. In our meetings with purveyors and managers of implementation sites, they were very clear that this can be a frustrating stage for those who are not prepared for it. The implementation-related activities intensify and resources are being spent, but "nothing is happening" with the students. In addition, funders and stakeholders can become impatient at this time, especially when more complex innovations are being implemented and months go by without seeing a lot of changes.

The installation stage is often overlooked, and there are few data about its role in successful implementation. In one of the few studies, Schaffer et al. (1997) conducted an analysis of issues that impede program implementation and sustainability, with regard to 10 promising education reform programs. The authors found that seed monies accepted by schools and districts for start-up costs related to the reform programs often were used to replenish needed resources and materials at the schools without the intention of actually implementing the program (another example of "paper implementation" as described in Chapter 2). The same study also showed that when programs required a heavy investment up front for such things as computers and contracts, the program was likely to continue to exist, whether or not the program was appropriate and producing good outcomes for the students. If it cost that much, they were going to continue doing it no matter what.

Conclusion: The installation stage is an important part of the implementation process. It should not be overlooked, nor should the investment of requisite resources be relied upon to *be* the program. Installation is a stage of implementation.

Initial Implementation

The initial implementation stage begins when students first experience some aspect of the innovation. Innovations are most vulnerable when they are being tried for the first time in a new education setting. Implementation requires change. The change may be more or less dramatic for a student, teacher, or school. Changes in skill levels, organizational capacity, organizational culture, and so on require training, practice, and time to mature. Joyce and Showers (2002) describe how they help teachers through the "initial awkward stage" of initial implementation. Fisher (1983) stated it clearly when he described "the real world ... [as] an environment full of personnel rules, social stressors, union stewards, anxious administrators, political pressures, interprofessional rivalry, staff turnover, and diamond-hard inertia" (p. 249). Given the complexity, change does not occur simultaneously or evenly in all parts of a practice or an organization.

In a review of 17 school reform programs, Protheroe (1998) noted several threats to implementation efforts (which begin in the initial implementation phase), including the need for sufficient time for teachers, staff, and administrators to learn new roles; increasing the quality of communication of everyone involved in the effort; preparing for new resources to support new training, content, and instructional strategies; recognizing the "achievement variability" that may occur, such as declines in test scores, as the new program is being implemented (p. 108); and working to reduce turnover and other factors that may create destabilizing change. The authors go on to stress that "Study after study of schools involved with comprehensive reform highlights the importance of realizing from the start the progress toward successful implementation will be difficult" (p. 107). The difficulties of first year implementation also were noted in the Rand evaluation of Edison Schools (an education management organization), where the authors emphasized that implementing the program takes time (a few years), as should be expected when implementing a comprehensive program (Gill et al., 2005).

In our practice reviews, it became clear that implementation of innovations almost always requires organizational change. That is, "To be effective, any design process must intentionally be, from the beginning, a redesign process" (Cawelti & Protheroe, 2003; Felner et al., 2001, p. 189; Fixsen et al., 1978; Kirkwood, Smith, & Tranfield, 1989; Phillips et al., 1978; Taylor, Nelson, & Adelman, 1999). Based on years of experience, Rosenheck (2001) sees that "Large human service organizations … are characterized by multiple and often conflicting goals, unclear and uncertain technologies for realizing those goals, and fluid participation and inconsistent attentiveness of principal actors. It is in this field of competition, ambiguity, and fluid managerial attention that efforts to import research findings into practice take place" (p. 1608). Thus, purveyors and other implementers find ways to help organizations (schools) change and grow to support and nourish innovations that benefit students.

Some innovations require more changes than others. For example, organizational supports were identified as critical by Felner et al. (2001), in their evaluation of the School Transitional Environment Project (STEP), a prevention and promotion program involving whole-school improvement and restructuring. The model seeks to modify the ecology of schools and schooling in order to build the principles of prevention and promotion into whole-school change.

It takes a number of years of effort to get full implementation that is associated with strong student gains. The focus of the STEP program is on structuring the physical environment by:

- Establishing small schools within large schools by assigning 60-100 students to a "team" and keeping students together in their classes to increase connectivity.
- Locating STEP classrooms in close proximity to each other, increasing the likelihood of students and teachers informally interacting and keeping students away from older students.

Teacher support is increased by:

- Expanding the role of the homeroom teacher so it is more comprehensive, taking on some of the roles of the guidance counselor (e.g., communication with parents, choosing classes, counseling), and linking to the rest of school and parents.
- Training and consultation for teachers with continuing supervision from school guidance staff, coupled with additional training for all in team building and student advisory skills.
- Regular team meetings and peer support among the STEP teachers in their team.

Across multiple trials, implementation of the STEP program was associated with clear declines in high school drop-out rates of 40-50% or more. STEP students also had lower levels of behavioral difficulties and were more likely to maintain academic performance and achievement levels. Common dimensions of high-performing schools included five interdependent components of implementation that need to be part of the implementation planning efforts of policy makers and practitioners:

1. Structural and organizational characteristics of schools (e.g., common planning time, class size, student-teacher ratios) were deemed to be "necessary, but certainly not sufficient, elements to obtain the gains in achievement and performance that were above those levels at which the student entered" (Felner et al., 2001, p. 189).
2. Attitudes, norms, and beliefs of staff; staff buy-in initially and over time.
3. Climate/empowerment/experiential characteristics (e.g., levels of stress, safety, feeling empowered to make decisions).
4. Capacity, skills, and knowledge teachers need to implement classroom changes.
5. Practice and procedural variables that can be used to build and convey high expectations throughout the school.

Implementation of a suicide prevention program required less organizational change since it involved a change in what was taught in a traditional classroom setting. However, a study of 33 of the 46 public high schools that had implemented the suicide prevention curriculum in one experimental county indicated that organizational supports were still critical (Kalafat & Ryerson, 1999). The results showed that, after the program had been implemented for several years, suicide rates for the state decreased modestly from 8.72 (5 years preimplementation) to 7.90 (5 years postimplementation), while the rates for the experimental county dropped dramatically from 7.26 to 4.38 during the same periods (pre to post). These schools were surveyed and key personnel interviewed about 10 years after implementation originally had been attempted. The survey found that about 80% of the schools had adopted written policies, and all but one continued to provide student education on suicide prevention. The interviews found that all the schools modified the suicide prevention curriculum to some degree, but only one change was to a core intervention component. In addition, all teachers using the program had received special training (many were still there, 10 years later) and felt that administrative support facilitated the program (time and scheduling, committed staff). The two schools that had dropped the program entirely lacked an in-school advocate. The trained coordinator left after 1 year in both schools, one principal left after the 1st year and the new principal did not support the program, and one faculty group was negative about the program.

Organizational changes were deemed to be important by Denton et al. (2003), who described taking research-based practice in reading intervention to scale. In their estimation, successful programs for students with learning disabilities (LD) are highly related to two factors:

1. The extent to which the general education teacher has the time, skills, knowledge, and interest in providing an appropriate education for students with LD.
2. The extent to which other personnel, such as the special education teachers, are able to control their schedules and case loads so that they are able to provide explicit and systematic instruction each day to a small group of students with LD (even if for only 45 minutes).

If either of these two factors is not in place, appropriate instruction in reading for students with LD is unlikely. Administrative support and leadership also seem to be closely related to the sustained use of an educational practice.

Conclusion: During the initial stage of implementation the compelling forces of fear of change, inertia, and investment in the status quo combine with the inherently difficult and complex work of implementing something new. In addition, all of this occurs at a time when the program is struggling to begin and when confidence in the decision to adopt the program is being tested. Attempts to implement new practices effectively may end at this point, overwhelmed by the proximal and distal influences on teachers and education leaders (e.g., Macallair & Males, 2004). Education leaders need to expect and prepare for changes in school policies, procedures, structures, roles, and duties in order to make effective use of innovations to benefit students.

Full Implementation

Implementation is synonymous with change. Most innovations require changes in teacher behavior and organizational changes in the school and district. That is why it is important that purveyors work with teachers, administrators, and other staff to achieve full implementation of an innovation. Full implementation of an innovation can occur once the new learning becomes integrated into teacher/administration, school, district, and community practices, policies, and procedures. At this point, the implemented program becomes fully operational with all of the realities of education influences impinging on the newly implemented innovation. Once an implemented program is fully operational, teachers and staff carry out the innovation with proficiency and skill, administrators support and facilitate the new practices, and parents and the community have embraced and adapted to the presence of the innovation. Some purveyors have developed "fidelity measures" to help assess the performance of teachers and others regarding their use of the innovation. A few purveyors also have established similar measures to assess the performance of the school as an organization, regarding its use of the innovation (see SFA and schoolwide PBS programs).

Over time, the innovation becomes accepted practice and a new operationalization of "treatment as usual" takes its place in the school and community (e.g. Faggin, 1985). The anticipated benefits should be realized at this point, as teachers and staff members become skillful and the procedures and processes become routinized. Once fidelity measures are above criterion levels most of the time, the effectiveness of the fully operational program implementation site should approximate the effectiveness of the original program.

Conclusion: It often takes 2 to 4 years to fully implement an education innovation. The core intervention components need to be used with fidelity and competence by teachers and staff. This almost always creates the need for changes in school structures and functions, with new roles and duties necessary to sustain the innovation and to continue to reap measurable benefits for students.

Innovation

Each attempted implementation of an innovation presents an opportunity to learn more about the program itself and the conditions under which it can be used with fidelity and good effect. New teachers and staff members working under different conditions within uniquely configured school and community circumstances present implementation challenges. They also present opportunities to refine and expand both the intervention practices and programs and the implementation practices and programs. Some of the changes at an implementation site will be undesirable and will be defined as program drift and a threat to fidelity (Adams, 1994; Mowbray, Holter, Teague, & Bybee, 2003; Yeaton & Sechrest, 1981). Others will be desirable changes and will be defined as innovations that need to be included in the "standard model" of treatment or implementation practices (Winter & Szulanski, 2001).

A common assumption when implementing education innovations is that the program will be adapted to meet local needs and resources and that this adaptation is a necessity (Datnow & Castellano, 2000; Denton et al., 2003; Elias et al., 2003; Fashola & Slavin, 1997; Han & Weiss, 2005; Slavin & Madden, 1999). However, while several researchers discussed the necessity of adaptation, many of these same researchers have found that, to achieve successful implementation of the program, the core components of the intervention must be defined and must not be adapted (Elias et al., 2003; Fashola & Slavin, 1997; Han & Weiss, 2005; Slavin & Madden, 1999). If adaptation of the core components of an intervention occurs, the intended program outcomes cannot be expected. Elias et al. (2003, p. 313) discuss how adaptations to the program must not cross into "the zone of drastic mutation," where the program no longer resembles the original innovation that was to be implemented (referred to here as program drift).

The best advice seems to be to implement the innovation with fidelity before attempting to innovate. In that way it is clear that "innovation" is not an attempt to escape the scrutiny of fidelity assessments and that the innovation is based on a skillful performance of the program or practice. In addition, Winter & Szulanski (2001) noted that adaptations made after an innovation had been implemented with fidelity were more successful than modifications made before full implementation. Innovations need to be evaluated to make sure they are adding value to the effectiveness of the innovation. Of course, at some point, innovations may sufficiently change the definition and operations of an evidence-based program to merit a new round of experimental outcome studies to confirm the overall benefits of the revised program.

To allow for appropriate adaptation at the classroom level, the SFA program utilizes a school site facilitator to guide teachers in decision making regarding proposed adaptation (one of the many activities of a site facilitator) (Datnow & Castellano, 2000; Slavin & Madden, 1999). The teachers discuss proposed adaptations and rationales for the changes with the site facilitator; through this process, the facilitator can determine if the adaptation would alter a core element of the program and provide alternatives for solving the teachers' problems without altering the program. This process has also helped the SFA program alter the core program itself, as teachers have made approved adaptations to the program that have proved beneficial to students and have been built into the core of the program.

Conclusion: First, implement the innovation with high degrees of fidelity and assess intended outcomes, then look at how to change the innovation in ways that better suit the needs of your school while maintaining or improving the outcomes.

Sustainability

Sustainability efforts begin during the exploration stage and never end. In our practice reviews, purveyors and implementers described how they began working with organizational leaders, funders, policy makers, and other key stakeholders soon after an organization expressed interest in implementing an innovation. Purveyors were not just passively assessing buy-in, fit, resources, motivation, and other key aspects of the exploration stage. They were also actively working to create more hospitable conditions to help ensure the successful implementation of the innovation at the school. These early contacts with key stakeholders help create the support necessary for initiating the innovation and for maintaining it over the long-term.

After an innovation is fully implemented in a new setting (often requiring 2 to 4 years), the work is not finished. Skilled teachers, administrators, and other well-trained staff leave and must be replaced. Leaders, funding streams, and program requirements change. New social problems arise; partners come and go. External systems change with some frequency, political alliances are only temporary, and champions move on to other causes. Through it all, the education leaders and staff, together with the community, must be aware of the shifting ecology of influence factors and adjust without losing the functional components of the program because of a lack of essential financial and political support. The goal during this stage is ensuring the long-term survival of the innovation and its continued benefits to students in the context of a changing world.

Conclusion: Sustainability of innovations over the long-term is important insofar as the benefits to students, schools, and communities continue to be apparent. Sustainability requires constant vigilance and continued attention to system supports, starting with the exploration stage and continuing through the life of the innovation.

Chapter 5

Implementation Drivers: From Staff Selection to Systems Intervention

Innovations are not like "plug and play" software that can be installed without much thought or preparation. Implementation of innovations is synonymous with change, and the implementation drivers are the core components of change at teacher, school, and district levels. The implementation drivers represent a way to think about, plan for, and evaluate implementation activities within any organization. The implementation drivers are based on the commonalities among successfully implemented innovations found in the literature and in practice. The use of innovations in education requires changes in how teachers conduct themselves in the classroom, changes in how administrators manage schools, and changes in the policies and funding practices of school districts.

The goal of implementation is to have teachers, staff, administrators, and policy makers base their interactions with consumers and stakeholders on innovations that have been demonstrated to be effective. To accomplish this, behavior change is created and supported by core implementation components (also called "implementation drivers"). The implementation drivers are shown in Figure 5.1. These core components are *staff selection, preservice and inservice training,*

Figure 5.1. Core Implementation Components for Successful Implementation of Education Innovations

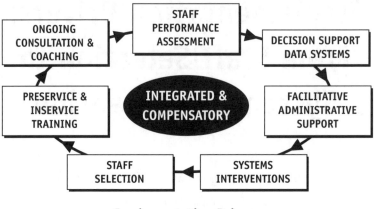

Implementation Drivers

ongoing consultation and coaching, staff performance assessment, decision support data systems, facilitative administrative support, and *systems interventions.* These interactive processes are integrated to maximize their influence on staff behavior and organizational culture. The interactive implementation drivers also compensate for one another, so that a weakness in one component can be overcome by strengths in other components.

The integrated and compensatory nature of the core implementation components represents a challenge for implementation and sustainability. Organizations are dynamic, so there is ebb and flow to the relative contribution of each component to the overall outcomes. The feedback loops are critical to keeping the innovation on track in the midst of a sea of change. If the feedback loops (i.e., staff performance assessments and decision support data systems) indicate needed changes, the integrated system needs to be adjusted to improve effectiveness or efficiency (see Bernfeld, 2001 for a more

Table 5.1. A Summary of a Meta-Analysis of the Effects of Training and Coaching on Teachers' Implementation in the Classroom			
	OUTCOMES (% of participants)		
Training Components	Demonstrate Knowledge	Demonstrate Skills in a Training Setting	Use New Skills in the Classroom
Theory and Discussion	10%	5%	0%
...+ Demonstration in Training	30%	20%	0%
...+ Practice & Feedback in Training	60%	60%	5%
...+ Coaching in Clinical Setting	95%	95%	95%

complete description of these interactive variables). That is, any changes in process or content in any one implementation driver require adjustments in other implementation drivers as well. Many well-run human service programs would fit the model shown in Figure 5.1. They are coherent, organized, mission-oriented, effective, and well evaluated.

The importance of integrated implementation drivers was illustrated by a meta-analysis of research on training and coaching carried out by Joyce and Showers (2002). They summarized several years of systematic research on training teachers in the public schools. As shown in Table 5.1, training that consisted only of theory and discussion produced a modest gain in knowledge and the ability of teachers to demonstrate the new skills in the protected training environment, but there was no transfer to the classroom. More substantial gains were made when demonstration, practice, and feedback were added to theory and discussion in a training workshop, but still with little use of the new skills in the classroom (Rogers, 2002, estimated that, in business, about 10% of what is taught in training is actually transferred to the job). When on-the-job coaching was added, large gains were seen in knowledge, ability to demonstrate the skills, and use of the new skills in the classroom with students. Joyce and Showers (2002) also noted that training and coaching can only be done with the full support and participation of school administrators (facilitative administration support), and works best with teachers who are willing and able to be fully involved (staff selection).

The descriptions of core implementation components (implementation drivers) are meant to provide a way to think about implementation. A given innovation may require more or less of any given component in order to be implemented successfully, and some innovations may be designed specifically to eliminate the need for one or more of the components (e.g., Baker, Gersten, & Keating, 2000; Embry, 2004). In addition, given the compensatory nature of the components, less training may be supplemented with greater amounts of coaching. Or, careful selection and very well-designed staff performance evaluations may compensate for less training and little coaching. However, when planning for implementation with fidelity and good effect for students and stakeholders, careful consideration should be given to each implementation driver.

Staff Selection

Staff selection is a key ingredient of implementation at every level (administrators, teachers, and staff). Who is qualified to carry out the education innovation? What are the methods for recruiting and selecting the teachers/staff who are most likely to be successful? Beyond academic qualifications or experience factors, certain characteristics are difficult to teach in training sessions, so they must be part of the selection criteria (e.g., knowledge of the field, common sense, social justice, ethics, willingness to learn, willingness to intervene, and good judgment). Some programs are purposefully designed to minimize the need for careful selection. For example, the SMART program for tutoring reading was designed to accept any adult volunteer who could read and was willing to spend 2 days a week tutoring a child (Baker et al., 2000). Other programs have specific requirements for practitioner qualifications (e.g., Chamberlain, 2003; Phillips, Burns, & Edgar, 2001; Schoenwald, Brown, & Henggeler, 2000) and competencies (e.g., Blase et al., 1984; Maloney, Phillips, Fixsen, & Wolf, 1975; Reiter-Lavery, 2004).

Staff selection in educational settings can be limited by several issues, including the level of autonomy the school has over hiring administrators, teachers, and staff; whether or not the teachers participate in a union or have teaching contracts with schools/districts; the differences in teaching certification requirements across states; and the variability in teaching and instructional strategies teachers receive at institutes of higher education (Bodilly, 1996; Denton et al., 2003; Gill et al., 2005). These factors greatly influence the level of control the school and/or district will have over selecting appropriate staff to be engaged in a new program. Several strategies have been described by researchers that facilitate staff selection at the school level. For example, Edison School programs require in their contracts with schools/districts that they be given the power to hire and fire teachers and principals (Gill et al., 2005). Having staffing authority over a school is seen as a core component of the program and is considered important, not only for implementation of the program, but also for obtaining staff buy-in. To align teachers, administrators, and staff with the Edison program, Edison maintains a national recruitment effort designed to select those who would be a good fit with the program. The Edison program seeks to hire staff based on the following defined selection criteria:

> Edison views the qualifications of applicants—whether teachers or principals—primarily in terms of expertise rather than years of experience. In principal candidates, Edison seeks a demonstrated track record of academic growth for students; the ability to talk to parents and achieve customer satisfaction; a commitment to the Edison program and the ability to get staff buy-in; familiarity with, ability to use, and understanding of the value of data; and strong financial management skills, including the ability to "think outside the box" in managing a budget. Principal candidates are asked to take an Edison-developed assessment to identify personal attributes, interests, attitudes, and behaviors, as well as strengths and weaknesses (Gill et al., 2005, p. 43).

If staffing authority cannot be achieved, schoolwide PBS and SFA programs require an endorsement from at least 80% of the teachers before beginning implementation (see the explanation of the exploration stage in Chapter 4). In addition, programs such as Edison and SFA work with schools and districts to ensure that teachers are given the option of voluntarily transferring to another school if they do not wish to participate in the new reform effort (Gill et al., 2005; Slavin & Madden, 1999). The voluntary transfer option is seen as a respectful way to allow teachers to choose whether or not to be in a setting with the new reform and allows schools to transfer staff that do not support the program (thereby increasing the potential for program success). In addition, if selection criteria for the program are in place, turnover of staff can be seen as an opportunity to hire staff more in line with the needs of the program. As Datnow and Castellano (2000) found in their qualitative case study of schools implementing the SFA program, principals were not pleased with turnover, but found that it gave them an opportunity to hire teachers that were knowledgeable about the program upfront and made an informed choice about working in the school's new environment.

Conclusion: Not every person is well suited (by temperament, abilities, or interests) for every innovation in education. Selection of teachers and other staff to carry out the core intervention components of an innovation is a key feature of successful implementation. It is another opportunity to play to the strengths of staff at each school.

Training

Innovations represent new ways of providing education. As part of the implementation of an innovation, teachers (and others) at a school need to learn when, where, how, and with whom to use new approaches and new skills. Preservice and inservice training are efficient ways to provide knowledge of background information, theory, philosophy, and values; introduce the components and rationales of key practices; and provide opportunities to practice new skills and receive feedback in a safe training environment. As shown in Table 5.1, most skills needed by successful practitioners can be introduced in training but are really learned on the job with the help of a consultant/coach (e.g., craft information, engagement, treatment planning, teaching to concepts, clinical judgment). Implementation of evidence-based practices requires behavior change at the practitioner, supervisory, and administrative support levels. Training and coaching are the principal ways in which behavior change is brought about for carefully selected staff in the beginning stages of implementation and throughout the life of evidence-based practices and programs.

While the content of training will vary considerably depending upon the education innovation that is being implemented, the methods of training seem to be less variable. There seem to be common approaches to imparting knowledge, skills, and abilities in programs to train teachers/practitioners (e.g., Bedlington, Booth, Fixsen, & Leavitt, 1996; Joyce & Showers, 2002; Schoenwald et al., 2000; Sparks, 2004), trainers (e.g., Braukmann & Blase, 1979; Ogden, Forgatch, Bullock, & Askeland, 2005), coaches (e.g., Joyce & Showers, 2002; Smart et al., 1979), fidelity evaluators (Davis, Warfel,

Maloney, Blase, & Fixsen, 1979; Wineman & Fixen, 1979), and administrators (Atherton, Mbekem, & Nyalusi, 1999; Baron, Watson, Coughlin, Fixsen, & Phillips, 1979). During training, information about history, theory, and philosophy, and rationales for program components and practices can be conveyed in lecture and discussion formats geared to knowledge acquisition and understanding. Skills and abilities related to carrying out the program components and practices can be demonstrated (live or taped), then followed by behavior rehearsal to practice the skills and receive feedback on the practice (Blase et al., 1984; Joyce & Showers, 2002; Kealey, Peterson, Gaul, & Dinh, 2000).

While they are not effective by themselves in producing change, training workshops are an efficient way to impart important information to practitioners and, when coupled with coaching, can contribute to important outcomes (e.g., Joyce & Showers, 2002). The meta-analysis of research studies carried out by Joyce and Showers (2002) indicates that effective training workshops appear to consist of presenting information (knowledge), providing demonstrations (live or taped) of the important aspects of the practice or program, and assuring opportunities to practice key skills in the training setting (behavior rehearsal). Some authors (Dreisbach, Luger, Ritter, & Smart, 1979; Dreisbach & Smart, 1980) noted the difference between role play ("Pretend you are someone else and try this") and behavior rehearsal ("You are in your position as a teacher and you are confronted with the following…"). Role plays might sharpen a teacher's understanding or empathy. Behavior rehearsals are direct preparation for the real thing and are meant to be as much like the education setting as possible. As found by Sparks (2004) in his review of staff development for teachers, training for new innovations and programs, especially large-scale programs, requires more than a day or two of training. Several programs needed 10-15 days. Sparks (2004) reminds us of the importance of coaching by noting that, while workshops are an important part of training, the more important piece is the learning that takes place as teachers implement the new program and "face the day-to-day challenges of their work" (p. 249).

Another interesting aspect of implementation has surfaced in our review of purveyors and their activities: the iterative nature of intervention and implementation content. For example, Sparks (2004) found that training and staff development strategies should incorporate the instructional strategies that teachers will be using with their students in implementing the new program. Sparks notes "…schools that want their students to be involved in more active forms of learning requiring the solving of real-life problems will provide learning opportunities for teachers that involve them in learning through similar means and producing comparable products" (p. 250). Solomon, Battistich, Watson, Schaps, and Lewis (2000) also found that training teachers through the same techniques to be used with students in the Child Development Project was important for staff development. Again, this points to the need to train teachers not only in the content of the program but also in the use of any new instructional strategies used with the new program. Fagan and Mihalic (2003) found in their study of the implementation of the Life Skills training program that, if teachers did not receive appropriate training in the new instructional strategies that accompanied the program, they would resort to didactic teaching of the program components, thereby reducing the potential outcomes of the program.

The effectiveness of training can be affected by several factors. Buston, Wight, Hart, and Scott (2002) evaluated the implementation of a sex education curriculum in Scottish schools. In the process of doing the study, they found that it was difficult to secure release time for teachers to participate in training, absences and turnover negatively affected availability for training, and role play was difficult for teachers. Joyce and Showers (2002) noted that new learning that is outside the experience of the trainee or requires a more complex repertoire of skills is more difficult for trainees to learn and master, and demands greater planning and precision from the trainers and coaches. Joyce and Showers (2002) also emphasized that the content of training must be useful and, ultimately, beneficial to consumers. They examined the teacher training content for one state and found that, even if implemented completely, only 5% of the content being taught to teachers was different enough from common practice to have any possible benefit to children. Education innovations that have well-defined core intervention components and good research support should be able to meet this criterion of potential benefit.

Conclusion: The essence of implementation is behavior change. Training by itself seems to be an ineffective approach to implementation. However, it appears that the functional components of staff training are knowledge of the program and practices, demonstrations of key skills, and practice to criterion of key skills. Special training for trainers and behavior rehearsal leaders may be required to maximize learning for the trainees. The essential aspects of training may be similar for imparting knowledge and skills to key organizational staff (staff, administrators) and teachers.

Staff Coaching

After a few decades of research on training teachers, Joyce and Showers (2002) began to think of training and coaching as one continuous set of operations designed to produce actual changes in the classroom behavior of teachers. Purveyors would agree: one without the other is insufficient. Behavior change is difficult for most people (for example, some people hire personal coaches to help them exercise more, change their eating behavior, or stop smoking). In their review of operations of ministries of health for the World Health Organization, Unger, Macq, Bredo, and Boelaert (2000) stated that implementing systems reform depends upon "training of field staff, on-the-spot expert coaching, and promotion of a new organizational structure." Spouse (2001) noted that formal knowledge ("episteme") needs to be supplemented with craft knowledge ("phronesis") so practitioners can learn to see how what they have learned is relevant to the situations at hand. Coaching needs to be work-based, opportunistic, readily available, and reflective (e.g., debriefing discussions). Spouse (2001) described four main roles of a coach:

- supervision
- teaching while engaged in practice activities
- assessment and feedback
- provision of emotional support

With newly learned behavior there are several simultaneous problems that must be faced:

1. *Newly learned behavior is crude compared to performance by a master practitioner.* Training usually is designed to introduce the learner to the essential elements of a new set of skills. For example, there are nine components of a "teaching interaction" (Phillips, Phillips, Fixsen, & Wolf, 1974), and these components are taught to and rehearsed by practitioners in a preservice training workshop until they reach mastery criteria (Kirigin et al., 1975). However, there are uncounted nuances of when and how to use the components in various combinations of proactive teaching, reactive teaching, conceptual teaching, effective praise, proactive prompting, etc., depending in part on the immediate behavior of particular children, families, or adults. This functional and adaptable set of skills is developed in practice with the help of a consultant/coach who shares craft knowledge as he or she observes, describes, and tutors the practitioner (Smart et al., 1979). With experience and effective coaching, a practitioner develops a personal style that is comfortable, while still incorporating the core intervention components of the evidence-based practice.

2. *Newly learned behavior is fragile and needs to be supported in the face of reactions from consumers and others in the service setting.* Behavior change directly affects others in the environment. For example, when a teacher makes a significant change in his or her behavior in the classroom, 20 to 30 children and their families react to that change. Joyce and Showers (2002) recommend having discussions with students and their parents to prepare them for the new ways of teaching that are about to be implemented.

   When practitioners change their behavior, the reactions from consumers and stakeholders initially may not be positive, effectively punishing the practitioner for making a change. For fragile, new behavior, the negative reaction may be enough to discourage the practitioner from persisting. One role of a coach is to prepare the practitioner for potential reactions and support the practitioner through the early stages of implementation until the new behavior is more skillfully embedded in the clinical environment (Joyce & Showers, 2002). Bierman et al. (2002), describe this as a counter-control function of a coach. That is, to help the practitioner engage in the new behavior, even though they are not yet proficient, despite the negative reactions to using the new behavior (sometimes poorly).

3. *Newly learned behavior is incomplete and will need to be shaped to be most functional in a service setting.* When designing workshop training experiences, there is only so much that can be accomplished effectively within the time available. Preservice workshop training can be used to develop entry-level knowledge and skills. Then, coaching can help teachers and others put the segmented basic knowledge and skills into the whole education context. Coaches can help teachers see how their personal beliefs and attitudes can be integrated with the skills, knowledge, philosophy, values, and principles of the program, as well as other aspects of the education context (Smart et al., 1979).

Additional Coaching Roles

In addition to helping establish new behavior in the education environment, emotional and personal support is another role for a coach (Spouse, 2001). In education, *teachers are the intervention*. Well-described innovations inform when and how they interact with students and stakeholders, but it is the person (the teacher) who delivers the intervention through his or her words and actions. In the transactional interplay between teacher and student, each affects the other in complex ways. For example, Fixsen and Blase (1993) pointed out that each dependent variable is also an independent variable in a treatment environment; in this case, the student is "teaching" the teacher, as well as being taught by the teacher.

It appears that the success of coaching is affected by several factors. Denton et al. (2003) reviewed attempts to implement reading programs for students with reading and learning disabilities. While noting that effective coaching was the most critical factor in successful implementation, they cautioned that effective coaching depended upon the availability of coaches who are expert in the content, techniques, and rationales of the program. It is said that good mentors are encouraging, supportive, committed, sensitive, flexible, respectful, enthusiastic, diplomatic, patient, and willing to share information, credit, and recognition (McCormick & Brennan, 2001). In their survey in Kentucky, McCormick and Brennan (2001) found that coaching was negatively affected by insufficient time allotted to do the work, reluctance to seek information from the mentor, role confusion due to the dual role of supervisor and coach, feelings of inadequacy on the part of the mentors, poor match between the coach and practitioner, and lack of availability of coaches in rural areas.

Joyce and Showers (2002) pointed out that leadership, organizational culture, labor relations, scheduling, interpersonal relationships, and engagement in participatory planning all affect the availability and effectiveness of coaching. In addition, coaches need to be trained to provide specialized coaching functions for teachers, and that requires more organizational leadership and more resources (Marks & Gersten, 1998). Furthermore, Showers and Joyce (1996) recommended that coaching relationships should start during training so parts of the training experience (practice new skills, receive feedback, repractice) can facilitate the development of the coaching relationship (a strategy also recommended by Smart et al., 1979).

Conclusion: As stated earlier, implementation of evidence-based practices and programs cannot occur unless teachers and other staff are well prepared to deliver the required practices in their interactions with students. Coaching makes clear contributions to the preparation of teachers. The core coaching components seem to be teaching and reinforcing evidence-based skill development and adaptations of skills and craft knowledge to fit the personal styles of the practitioners (changing form, not function).

Staff Performance Assessment

Staff performance assessment is designed to assess the use and outcomes of the skills that are reflected in the selection criteria, taught in training, and reinforced and expanded in consultation and coaching processes. Assessments of practitioner performance and measures of fidelity also provide useful feedback to school leaders and purveyors regarding the progress of implementation efforts and the usefulness of training and coaching. Staff evaluation and fidelity consist of some combination of measures of context, compliance, and competence (Forgatch, Patterson, & DeGarmo, 2005; Waltz, Addis, Koerner, & Jacobson, 1993). With respect to these measures:

- Context refers to the prerequisites that must be in place for a program or practice to operate (e.g., staffing qualifications or numbers, practitioner-consumer ratio, supervisor-practitioner ratio, location of service provision, prior completion of training).
- Compliance refers to the extent to which the practitioner uses the core intervention components prescribed by the evidence-based program or practice and avoids those proscribed by the program or practice.
- Competence refers to the level of skill shown by the practitioner in using the core intervention components as prescribed, while delivering the treatment to a consumer.

In a highly functional system, staff evaluation is part of a sequence of supports designed to have good people well prepared to do an effective job. In these cases, assessments of performance are well integrated with what has been taught and coached, and there are no surprises for the teacher or other staff. The feedback from more formalized assessments also provides information for the coaching process (Davis, Warfel, Maloney, Blase, & Fixsen,1978; Phillips et al., 1974; Schoenwald et al., 2000; Smart et al., 1979) and is an outcome measure for the quality of coaching (Blase et al., 1984; Schoenwald et al., 2004).

The effectiveness of staff performance evaluation may be affected by several factors. McGrew, Bond, Dietzen, and Salyers (1994) noted that the development of fidelity measures often is hampered in three ways: (1) most program models are not well defined conceptually, making it difficult to identify core intervention components, (2) when core intervention components have been identified, they are

not operationally defined with agreed-upon criteria for implementation, and (3) only a few models have been around long enough to
study planned and unplanned variations. In addition, staff evaluations need to be practical so they can be done routinely in an organization (Blase et al., 1984; Henggeler, Melton, Brondino, Scherer,
& Hanley, 1997), and staff evaluators need to be prepared for their
roles. Given the integrated nature of any organization, it is likely that
administrative decisions, changes in budget, office moves, etc. can
have unintended and undesirable effects on teacher behavior and,
therefore, affect fidelity.

Conclusion: The best intervention will not produce positive effects
if it is not implemented correctly. Thus, assessments of performance
are a critical component of implementation. Context fidelity measures describe the necessary precursors to high-level performance
(e.g., completion of training, availability of colleagues with special
skills, availability of certain resources) for a particular program or
practice. Compliance fidelity measures provide an outline of the core
intervention components and their use by the practitioner. Competence fidelity measures are essential for determining the extent to
which the core intervention components were delivered with skill
and attention to the craft when interacting with students and stakeholders. The results of fidelity measures and staff evaluations seem
to have many practical uses. Coaches can use the information to
sharpen their professional development agendas with practitioners.
Administrators can use the information to assess the quality of training and coaching. Purveyors can use the information as a guide for
implementation at the practice and program development levels.
And researchers can use the information as an outcome measure for
some studies and as an independent variable in others.

Decision Support Data Systems

Decision support data systems (DSDS) (e.g., quality improvement information, organizational fidelity measures) assess key aspects of the overall performance of the organization to help ensure continuing implementation of the core intervention components over time. Having reliable data available is an important first step. However, the essence of DSDS is using the data to make decisions that help improve the educational outcomes for students and stakeholders. SFA, Edison Schools, schoolwide PBS, and other education innovations have well-developed data systems and methods to help teachers, administrators, district staff, and others use the data to facilitate decision making. For example, the schoolwide PBS purveyors help schools use the schoolwide evaluation tool to assess changes in school functioning and sustain the use of PBS (Horner & Sugai, 2005).

Solomon et al. (2000) describe the use of an Index of Implementation in evaluating teacher fidelity in the Child Development Project (CDP) program. The CDP is a whole-school reform program that focuses on creating a supported learning community in elementary schools to foster relationships, focus on the needs of students, and promote prosocial behaviors. In a study assessing the effect of the CDP program across six school districts, the researchers developed an Index of Implementation to monitor fidelity that included both a teacher observation protocol and a teacher questionnaire. The observation protocol was completed during four time periods over the school year for all 24 schools participating in the study (both those receiving the program and the comparison schools). The observation protocol included 6 scales (62 items total) and a 3-point rating scale was utilized to rate the items. The teacher questionnaire, used to assess teacher's beliefs and attitudes each spring, was an adapted questionnaire which focused only on items that would be important for program implementation. By collecting data on program implementation, the researchers were able to distinguish between those schools that were receiving the program and implementing well, and those schools that were not (with only 5 of 12 progressing on implementation). In addition, the researchers were able to link student outcomes with levels of program implementation, finding that "...*program status* (program vs. comparison school) led to increases over the four years in *program implementation*, that increases in *program implementation* led to increases in student's *sense of community*, and that increases in *sense of community*, in turn, led to increases in most of the assessed *student outcomes*" (Solomon et al., 2000, p.26). Furthermore, in a paper discussing the detailed use of the Index of Implementation in the CDP program in the six school districts, Battisitch (1999) stresses the importance of the teacher implementation evaluation data, stating "Absent implementation data, the conclusions of the study would be one of program ineffectiveness" (p. 3).

Facilitative Administration

If the teacher is the intervention in education, the function of the administration is to actively and creatively support the high fidelity work of the teacher. Facilitative administrators are eager to find new ways to reduce barriers and provide more resources to help teachers make maximum use of innovative education practices to benefit students and stakeholders. Facilitative administration provides leadership and makes use of a range of data inputs to inform decision making, support the overall processes, and keep staff organized and focused on the desired educational outcomes.

As noted earlier, the implementation drivers are integrated and compensatory. That is, the drivers are all related to one another, and gaps or weaknesses in one driver may be compensated for by strengths in another (an example would be the need for strong coaching strategies to compensate for weak training strategies). McGuire (2001) underscores the importance of staff selection, staff training, staff coaching, and facilitative administrative supports by stating that

> [E]ven well-designed intervention programmes (sic) may have nil and possibly even negative effects if the quality of delivery is poor....There are no known treatment or training materials that will achieve their goals in the absence of trained and committed staff with adequate resources and managerial support (p. 34).

As mentioned previously, a study of the New American Schools Demonstration Phase (Bodilly, 1996) focused on the implementation strategies used across programs. During focus group follow-ups with teachers and administrators participating in the reform programs, several key strategies of program developers were delineated that were considered key to implementation (including those for training, facilitative administrative support for teachers, identified core components, etc.). However, the teachers, administrators, and program developers felt that the components of the strategy could "substitute" for one another, allowing for a weakness in one (such as training) to be compensated by the strength of another (such as detailed descriptions of core program components).

Conclusion: There is no such thing as an "administrative decision." They are all education decisions that affect how much time, energy, and skill teachers and others will bring to the educational experience of students. It is up to school and district administrators to ensure proper supports for teachers and others who are doing the skillful work of innovative education.

System Intervention

No matter how good the program may be, if national policy changes and certain services are no longer funded, those services will disappear. Without hospitable leadership and organizational structures, core intervention components cannot be installed and maintained. Without adequate pay, skillful teachers and administrators will be hard to find and keep, and programs will falter. Like gravity, organizational and external influence variables seem to be omnipresent and influential at all levels of implementation. Systems interventions are strategies to work with external systems to ensure the availability of the financial, organizational, and human resources required to support the work of teachers using innovations in education. In this regard, a critical component of successful implementation is helping to establish and maintain alignment of external influences and resources with the needs of education innovations, both during the active implementation stages and the longer-term sustainability stage.

The potential relationships among core implementation components, organizational features, and influence factors are shown in Figure 5.2. Various authors (Bernfeld, Blase, & Fixsen, 1990; Bernfeld, Farrington, & Leschied, 2001; Edwards, Schoenwald, Henggeler, & Strother, 2001; Kirby et al., 2001; Morton, 1991; Paine et al., 1984; Salasin & Davis, 1977; Schoenwald & Hoagwood, 2001) have described a similar multilevel approach to understanding the transactional effects shared by these domains. As discussed earlier, the

Figure 5.2. Multilevel Influences on Successful Implementation

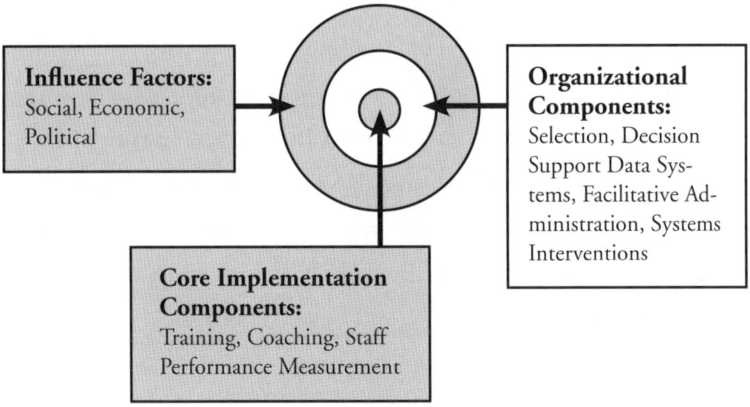

Influence Factors:
Social, Economic, Political

Organizational Components:
Selection, Decision Support Data Systems, Facilitative Administration, Systems Interventions

Core Implementation Components:
Training, Coaching, Staff Performance Measurement

core implementation components appear to be essential to changing the behavior of teachers, staff, and other personnel who are key providers of innovations within a school. The core components do not exist in a vacuum. They are contained within and supported by an organization that establishes facilitative administrative structures and processes to select, train, coach, and evaluate the performance of practitioners and other key staff members; develops decision support data systems; and intervenes in external systems to ensure ongoing resources and support for the innovative practices used within the school. Thus, as shown in Figure 5.2, the core implementation components must be present for implementation to occur with fidelity and good outcomes. The organizational components must be present to enable and support those core components over the long-term. And, all of this must be accomplished over the years in the context of capricious but influential changes in governments, leadership, funding priorities, economic boom-bust cycles, shifting social priorities, and so on (e.g. Kirby et al., 2001).

We postulate that our understanding of the contributions of organizational and external influences on the effectiveness of core implementation components will be furthered when all three levels are measured simultaneously. For example, Klinger, Ahwee, Pilonieta, and Menendez (2003) noted a linear relationship between implementation and administrative support for teachers learning new instructional methods for inclusive classrooms. That is, when teachers perceived that the instructional practice was valued by their school leader, there was a greater likelihood they would implement the practice. However, Gersten, Chard, and Baker (2000) suggest that teachers who have developed a high degree of mastery of an innovation may be able to persevere in their implementation despite changes in administration. Thus, organizational factors may have a greater effect on new learning and less of an effect on well-established repertoires and routines. It seems likely that the desired outcomes of sustainable high fidelity practices will be best achieved when strong core implementation components are well supported by strong organizational structures and cultures in an enabling mix of external influences.

All of this means that education leaders need to keep the external influence factors in mind as they implement innovations in schools. Some pervasive external influence factors identified in the literature include federal and state laws, local ordinances, departmental administrative policies, funding priorities, community resources, interests of local consumers, and advocates' concerns (Corrigan, 2001; Zins & Illback, 1995). It has been noted that, "Successful implementers carefully monitored entire change processes, regulating and controlling social and political issues as they arose" (Neufeld & Roper, 2003, p. 255). It is up to school and district administrators to monitor these external influences and continue to work to help ensure adequate support for the use of innovative practices in the education environment. In our discussions with program directors and administrators, the lack of alignment usually comes to light after the fact, when they find that new policies, etc. are hindering the teachers'/schools' abilities to carry out the innovative education practices. They then go to work to reduce the barriers and create new facilitators so the innovation can continue to thrive for the benefit of students.

Conclusion: The literature suggests that core implementation components, organizational components, and influence factors interact to produce implementation outcomes. Core implementation components exist in the context of organizational and influence factors that can support or hinder their availability, operations, and effectiveness. The literature is helpful in pointing out areas of influence and candidates for systems intervention in order to successfully implement and sustain programs and practices over the long-term.

Chapter 6
Conclusions

Research-based solutions to many issues facing educators are in the literature and waiting to be implemented successfully in schools across the nation. The current science-to-service gap (the "quality chasm" referenced by the Institute of Medicine, 2001) provides painful evidence of the difficulties involved in successful implementation of innovations in human service fields, including education. Our reviews of the literature and current practices point to implementation as the missing link in the science-to-service chain.

Implementation is the art and science of moving research-based innovations into practice in order to achieve the promised benefits to students, schools, and communities. Thanks to the persistence of purveyors and researchers in the field, we now have enough information to put the puzzle pieces together to construct a theory of implementation (the frameworks provided in this book) to guide future practice and research. The stages of implementation and the implementation drivers provide guideposts for education leaders as they make plans for the next round of education improvements and school reform initiatives.

We now know that our most widely used methods for attempting implementation do *not* work with respect to implementation of innovations:

- Information dissemination alone (research literature, mailings, promulgation of practice guidelines) is an ineffective implementation method.
- Training (no matter how well done) by itself is an ineffective implementation method.

It appears that successful implementation efforts designed to achieve beneficial outcomes for consumers require a longer-term multilevel approach. The literature and practice reviews provide evidence related to innovation-specific practitioner selection, skill-based training, innovation-specific coaching, practitioner performance evaluation, decision support data systems, facilitative administrative practices, and methods for systems interventions. The task of aligning system and organizational structures with desired practices seems to be a continuous one that engages policy makers, state planners, education leaders, and purveyors of innovations. Frameworks for trying to understand the relationships among system, organizational, and practice variables were presented as a possible guide to planners and purveyors.

Perhaps the most noticeable gap in the available literature concerns interaction effects among implementation factors and their relative influences over time. Tantalizing tidbits have been provided in recent studies by Felner et al. (2001), Fixsen et al. (2001), Joyce and Showers (2002), Khatri and Frieden (2002), Panzano et al. (2005), and Schoenwald et al. (2003, 2004). These authors have begun a process to carefully evaluate the various links among implementation stages, implementation components, and purveyor approaches with adoption rates, program and practitioner effectiveness, and implementation site sustainability as the dependent measures. However, analyzing interaction effects is a difficult task, given the sheer number of implementation variables identified as important in this review. The study of interaction effects over time will require planning among researchers, policy makers, federal and state funders, and purveyor groups to develop a multiyear program of research to tease out the most useful combinations of factors at each stage of innovation implementation.

In the meantime, the frameworks presented in this book can provide guidance for successful implementation of education innovations to benefit students, schools, and communities.

References

Adams, P. (1994). Marketing social change: The case of family preservation. *Children and Youth Services Review, 16*, 417-431.

Arthur, M. W., & Blitz, C. (2000). Bridging the gap between science and practice in drug abuse prevention through needs assessment and strategic community planning. *Journal of Community Psychology, 28*(3), 241-255.

Atherton, F., Mbekem, G., & Nyalusi, I. (1999). Improving service quality: Experience from the Tanzania Family Health Project. *International Journal for Quality in Health Care, 11*(4), 353-356.

Baker, S., Gersten, R., & Keating, T. (2000). When less may be more: A 2-year longitudinal evaluation of a volunteer tutoring program requiring minimal training. *Reading Research Quarterly, 35*(4), 494-519.

Baron, R. L., Watson, D. M., Coughlin, D. D., Fixsen, D. L., & Phillips, E. L. (1979). *The program manager training manual.* Boys Town, NE: Father Flanagan's Boys' Home.

Battistich, V. (1999). *Assessing implementation of the child development project.* Paper presented at the Implementation Research in School-Based Models of Prevention and Promotion, Pennsylvania State University, State College, PA.

Bauman, L. J., Stein, R. E. K., & Ireys, H. T. (1991). Reinventing fidelity: The transfer of social technology among settings. *American Journal of Community Psychology, 19*, 619-639.

Becker, W. C., & Engelmann, S. (1995). Sponsor findings from Project Follow Through. *Effective School Practices, 15*(1).

Bedlington, M., Booth, C., Fixsen, D., & Leavitt, S. (1996). *Skills for family and community living: A guidebook for practitioners.* Federal Way, WA: Behavioral Sciences Institute.

Beer, M., Eisenstat, R. A., & Spector, B. (1990). Why change programs don't produce change. *Harvard Business Review, 68*(6), 158-166.

Bernfeld, G. A. (2001). The struggle for treatment integrity in a "dis-integrated" service delivery system. In G. A. Bernfeld, D. P. Farrington, & A. W. Leschied (Eds.), *Offender rehabilitation in practice: Implementing and evaluating effective programs* (pp. 167-188). London: Wiley.

Bernfeld, G. A., Blase, K. B., & Fixsen, D. L. (1990). Towards a unified perspective on human service delivery systems: Application of the teaching-family model. In R. J. McMahon & R. D. V. Peters (Eds.), *Behavior disorders of adolescents: Research, intervention and policy in clinical and school settings.* (pp. 191-205). New York: Plenum Press.

Bernfeld, G. A., Farrington, D. P., & Leschied, A. W. (2001). Offender rehabilitation in practice: Implementing and evaluating effective programs. New York: John Wiley & Sons Ltd.

Bierman, K. L., Coie, J. D., Dodge, K. A., Greenberg, M. T., Lochman, J. E., McMahon, R. J., et al. (2002). The implementation of the Fast Track Program: An example of a large-scale prevention science efficacy trial. *Journal of Abnormal Child Psychology, 30*(1), 1-17.

Blase, K. A., & Fixsen, D. L. (2003). *Evidence-based programs and cultural competence*. Tampa, FL: National Implementation Research Network, Louis de la Parte Florida Mental Health Institute, University of South Florida.

Blase, K. A., Fixsen, D. L., & Phillips, E. L. (1984). Residential treatment for troubled children: Developing service delivery systems. In S. C. Paine, G. T. Bellamy, & B. Wilcox (Eds.), *Human services that work: From innovation to standard practice* (pp. 149-165). Baltimore: Paul H. Brookes Publishing.

Bodilly, S. (1996). *Lessons from the New American Schools Development Corporation's demonstration phase.* Santa Monica, CA: Institute on Education and Training, RAND Corporation.

Braukmann, C. J., & Blase, K. B. (Ed.). (1979). *Teaching-Parent training manual (2 vols.).* Lawrence, KS: University of Kansas Printing Service.

Buston, K., Wight, D., Hart, G., & Scott, S. (2002). Implementation of a teacher-delivered sex education programme: Obstacles and facilitating factors. *Health Education Research, 17*(1), 59-72.

Cawelti, G., & Protheroe, N. (2003). *Supporting school improvement: Lessons from districts successfully meeting the challenge.* Arlington, VA: Educational Research Service.

Chamberlain, P. (2003). The Oregon Multidimensional Treatment Foster Care Model: Features, outcomes, and progress in dissemination. *Cognitive and Behavioral Practice, 10,* 303-312.

Cheung, W. M., & Cheng, Y. C. (1997). The strategies for implementing multilevel self-management in schools. *International Journal of Educational Management, 11*(4), 159-169.

Cooper, R., Slavin, R. E., & Madden, N. A. (1998). Success for All: Improving the quality of implementation of whole-school change through the use of a national reform network. *Education and Urban Society, 30*(3), 385-408.

Corrigan, P. W. (2001). Strategies for disseminating evidence-based practices to staff who treat people with serious mental illness. *Psychiatric Services, 52*(12), 1598-1606.

Dale, N., Baker, A. J. L., & Racine, D. (2002). *Lessons learned: What the WAY Program can teach us about program replication.* Washington, DC: American Youth Policy Forum.

Datnow, A., & Castellano, M. (2000). *An inside look at Success for All: A qualitative study of the implementation and teaching and learning* (Report No. 45). Baltimore: Johns Hopkins University, Center for Research on the Education of Students Placed at Risk.

Davis, M., Warfel, D. J., Maloney, D. M., Blase, K. B., & Fixsen, D. L. (1979). *Consumer evaluation manual: How to assess consumer attitudes towards group homes* (2nd ed.). Boys Town, NE: Father Flanagan's Boys' Town.

Denton, C. A., Vaughn, S., & Fletcher, J. M. (2003). Bringing research-based practice in reading intervention to scale. *Learning Disabilities Research & Practice, 18*(3), 201-211.

Dreisbach, L., & Smart, D. J. (1980). *The preservice workshop producer's manual.* Boys Town, NE: Father Flanagan's Boys' Home.

Dreisbach, L., Luger, R., Ritter, D., & Smart, D. J. (1979). *The confederate role workshop: Trainer's manual.* Boys Town, NE: Father Flanagan's Boys' Home.

Edwards, D. L., Schoenwald, S. K., Henggeler, S. W., & Strother, K. B. (2001). A multi-level perspective on the implementation of multisystemic therapy (MST): Attempting dissemination with fidelity. In G. A. Bernfeld, D. Farrington, & A. W. Lescheid (Eds.), *Offender rehabilitation in practice: Implementing and evaluating effective programs*. New York: John Wiley & Sons Ltd.

Elias, M. J., Zins, J. E., Graczyk, P.A., & Weissberg, R. P. (2003). Implementation, sustainability, and scaling up of social-emotional and academic innovations in public schools. *School Psychology Review, 32*(3), 303-319.

Elliott, D. S., & Mihalic, S. (2004). Issues in disseminating and replicating effective prevention programs. *Prevention Science, 5*(1), 47-52.

Ellis, P., Robinson, P., Ciliska, D., Armour, T., Raina, P., Brouwers, M., et al. (2003). *Diffusion and dissemination of evidence-based cancer control interventions*. (Evidence Report/Technology Assessment No. 79. AHRQ Publication No. 03-E033). Rockville, MD: Agency for Healthcare Research and Quality.

Embry, D. D. (2004). Community-based prevention using simple, low-cost, evidence-based kernels and behavior vaccines. *Journal of Community Psychology, 32*(5), 575-591.

Fagan, A. A., & Mihalic, S. (2003). Strategies for enhancing the adoption of school-based prevention programs: Lessons learned from the blueprints for violence prevention replications of the Life Skills training program. *Journal of Community Psychology, 31*(3), 235-253.

Faggin, F. (1985). The challenge of bringing new ideas to market. *High Technology*, 14-16.

Fairweather, G. W., Sanders, D. H., & Tornatzky, L. G. (1974). Principles for creating change in mental health organizations. In *Creating change in mental health organizations* (pp. 181-197). Elmsford, NY: Pergamon Press.

Fashola, O. S., & Slavin, R. E. (1997). *Effective and replicable programs for students placed at risk in elementary and middle schools*: Paper written under funding from the Office of Educational Research and Improvement. Baltimore: John Hopkins University.

Feldman, S., Baler, S., & Penner, S. (1997). The role of private-for-profit managed behavioral health in the public sector. *Administration and Policy in Mental Health, 24,* 379-390.

Felner, R. D., Favazza, A., Shim, M., Brand, S., Gu, K., & Noonan, N. (2001). Whole school improvement and restructuring as prevention and promotion: Lessons from STEP and the project on high performance learning communities. *Journal of School Psychology, 39*(2), 177-202.

Fisher, D. (1983). The going gets tough when we descend from the ivory tower. *Analysis and Intervention in Developmental Disabilities, 3*(2-3 SU), 249-255.

Fitzgerald, L., Ferlie, E., & Hawkins, C. (2003). Innovation in healthcare: How does credible evidence influence professionals? *Health & Social Care in the Community, 11*(3), 219.

Fixsen, D. L., & Blase, K. A. (1993). Creating new realities: Program development and dissemination. *Journal of Applied Behavior Analysis, 26,* 597-615.

Fixsen, D. L., Blase, K. A., Timbers, G. D., & Wolf, M. M. (2001). In search of program implementation: 792 replications of the Teaching-Family Model. In G. A. Bernfeld, D. P. Farrington & A. W. Leschied (Eds.), *Offender rehabilitation in practice: Implementing and evaluating effective programs* (pp. 149-166). London: Wiley.

Fixsen, D. L., Naoom, S. F., Blase, K.A., Friedman, R.M., & Wallace, F. (2005). *Implementation research: A synthesis of the literature* (FMHI Publication No. 231). Tampa, FL: University of South Florida, Louis de la Parte Florida Mental Health Institute, The National Implementation Research Network. (http://nirn.fmhi.usf.edu/resources/publications/Monograph/index.cfm)

Fixsen, D. L., Phillips, E. L., & Wolf, M. M. (1978). Mission-oriented behavior research: The Teaching-Family Model. In A. C. Catania & T. A. Brigham (Eds.), *Handbook of applied behavior analysis: Social and instructional processes* (pp. 603-628). New York: Irvington Publishers, Inc.

Forgatch, M. S., Patterson, G. R., & DeGarmo, D. S. (2005). Evaluating fidelity: predictive validity for a measure of competent adherence to the Oregon model of parent management training. *Behavior Therapy, 36*(1), 3-13.

Fox, J., & Gershman, J. (2000). The World Bank and social capital: Lessons from ten rural development projects in the Philippines and Mexico. *Policy Sciences, 33*(3-4), 399-419.

Gendreau, P., Goggin, C., & Smith, P. (1999). The forgotten issue in effective correctional treatment: Program implementation. *International Journal of Offender Therapy and Comparative Criminology, 43*(2), 180-187.

Gersten, R., Chard, D., & Baker, S. (2000). Factors enhancing sustained use of research-based instructional practices. *Journal of Learning Disabilities, 33,* 445-457.

Gill, B. P., Hamilton, L. S., Lockwood, J. R., Marsh, J. A., Zimmer, R. W., Hill, D., et al. (2005). *Inspiration, perspiration, and time: Operations and achievement in Edison schools.* Santa Monica, CA: RAND Corporation.

Goggin, M. L. (1986). The "too few cases/too many variables" problem in implementation research. *The Western Political Quarterly, 39*(2), 328-347.

Greenhalgh, T., Robert, G., MacFarlane, F., Bate, P., & Kyriakidou, O. (2004). Diffusion of innovations in service organizations: Systematic review and recommendations. *The Milbank Quarterly, 82*(4), 581-629.

Han, S. S., & Weiss, B. (2005). Sustainability of teacher implementation of school-based mental health programs. *Journal of Abnormal Child Psychology, 33*(6), 665-679.

Havelock, R. G., & Havelock, M. C. (1973). *Training for change agents.* Ann Arbor, MI: University of Michigan Institute for Social Research.

Haynes, N. M., Emmons, C. L., Gebreyesus, S., Ben-Avie, M. (1996). The school development program evaluation process. In *Rallying the whole village: The Comer process for reforming education* (pp. 123-146). New York: Teachers College.

Henggeler, S. W., Melton, G. B., Brondino, M. J., Scherer, D. G., & Hanley, J. H. (1997). Multisystemic therapy with violent and chronic juvenile offenders and their families: The role of treatment fidelity in successful dissemination. *Journal of Consulting and Clinical Psychology, 65*(5), 821-833.

Horner, R. H., & Sugai, G., (2005). School-wide Positive Behavior Support: An alternative approach to discipline in schools. In L. Bambara & L. Kern (Eds.) *Positive Behavior Support.* New York: Guilford Press.

Institute of Medicine—Committee on Quality of Health Care in America. (2001). *Crossing the quality chasm: A new health system for the 21st century.* Washington, DC: National Academy Press.

Joyce, B., & Showers, B. (2002). *Student achievement through staff development* (3rd ed.). Alexandria, VA: Association for Supervision and Curriculum Development.

Kalafat, J., & Ryerson, D. M. (1999). The implementation and institutionalization of a school-based youth suicide prevention program. *Journal of Primary Prevention, 19*(3), 157-175.

Kam, C., Greenberg, M. T., & Kusché, C. A. (2004). Sustained effects of the PATHS curriculum on the social and psychological adjustment of children in special education. *Journal of Emotional and Behavioral Disorders, 12,* 66-78.

Kealey, K. A., Peterson, A. V., Jr., Gaul, M. A., & Dinh, K. T. (2000). Teacher training as a behavior change process: Principles and results from a longitudinal study. *Health Education & Behavior, 27*(1), 64-81.

Khatri, G. R., & Frieden, T. R. (2002). Rapid DOTS expansion in India. *Bulletin of the World Health Organization, 80*(6), 457-463.

Kirby, S. N., Berends, M., & Naftel, S. (2001*). Implementation in a longitudinal sample of new American schools: Four years into scale-up.* Santa Monica, CA: RAND Corporation.

Kirigin, K. A., Ayala, H. E., Braukmann, C. J., Brown, W. G., Minkin, N., Fixsen, D. L., et al. (1975). Training teaching-parents: An evaluation of workshop training procedures. In E. Ramp & G. Semb (Eds.), *Behavior analysis: Areas of research and application* (pp. 161-174). Englewood Cliffs, NJ: Prentice-Hall.

Kirkwood, R., Smith, S., & Tranfield, D. (1989). The implementation cube for advanced manufacturing systems. *International Journal of Operations and Production Management, 9*(8).

Klingner, J. K., Ahwee, S., Pilonieta, P., & Menendez, R. (2003). Barriers and facilitators in scaling up research-based practices. *Exceptional Children, 69*(4), 411-429.

Knoff, H. (2005). *Project ACHIEVE overview and briefing document.* Little Rock, AR: Arkansas Department of Education.

Kraft, J. M., Mezoff, J. S., Sogolow, E. D., Neumann, M. S., & Thomas, P. A. (2000). A technology transfer model for effective HIV/AIDS interventions: Science and practice. *AIDS Education and Prevention, 12*(Supplement A), 7-20.

Macallair, D., & Males, M. (2004). A failure of good intentions: An analysis of juvenile justice reform in San Francisco during the 1990s. *Review of Policy Research, 21*(1), 63-78.

Maloney, D. M., Phillips, E. L., Fixsen, D. L., & Wolf, M. M. (1975). Training techniques for staff in group homes for juvenile offenders. *Journal of Criminal Justice and Behavior, 2,* 195-216.

Marks, S. U., & Gersten, R. (1998). Engagement and disengagement between special and general educators: An application of miles and Huberman's cross-case analysis. *Learning Disability Quarterly, 21*(1), 34-56.

McCormick, K. M., & Brennan, S. (2001). Mentoring the new professional in interdisciplinary early childhood education: The Kentucky Teacher Internship Program. *Topics in Early Childhood Special Education, 21*(3), 131-144.

McGrew, J. H., Bond, G. R., Dietzen, L., & Salyers, M. (1994). Measuring the fidelity of implementation of a mental health program model. *Journal of Consulting & Clinical Psychology, 62*(4), 670-678.

McGuire, J. (2001). What works in correctional intervention? Evidence and practical implications. In G. A. Bernfeld, D. P. Farrington, & A. W. Leschied (Eds.), *Offender rehabilitation in practice: Implementing and evaluating effective programs* (pp. 25-43). London: Wiley.

Mihalic, S., & Irwin, K. (2003). Blueprints for violence prevention: From research to real-world settings—factors influencing the successful replication of model programs. *Youth Violence and Juvenile Justice, 1*(4), 307-329.

Morton, M. S. S. (1991). *The corporation of the 1990s: Information technology and organizational transformation.* New York: Oxford University Press.

Mowbray, C. T., Holter, M. C., Teague, G. B., & Bybee, D. (2003). Fidelity criteria: Development, measurement, and validation. *American Journal of Evaluation, 24*(3), 315-340.

Neufeld, B., & Roper, D. (2003). *Coaching: A strategy for developing instructional capacity.* Cambridge, MA: Education Matters, Inc.

Nutt, P. C. (2002). *Why Decisions Fail.* San Francisco: Berrett Kochler Publishers.

Ogden, T., Forgatch, M. S., Bullock, B. M., & Askeland, E. (2005). Large scale implementation of parent management training at the national level: The case of Norway. *Journal of Social Work Practice, 19*(3), 317-329.

Paine, S. C., Bellamy, G. T., & Wilcox, B. L. (Eds.). (1984). *Human services that work: From innovation to standard practice.* Baltimore: Paul H. Brookes.

Panzano, P. C., Seffrin, B., Chaney-Jones, S., Roth, D., Crane-Ross, D., Massatti, R., et al. (2005). The innovation diffusion and adoption research project (IDARP): Moving from the diffusion of research results to promoting the adoption of evidence-based innovations in the Ohio mental health system. *New Research in Mental Health, 16,* 78-89.

Phillips, E. L., Baron, R. L., Daly, D. L., Daly, P. B., Evans, J. H., & Fixsen, D. L. (1978). *Program development, staff training, and practical evaluation at Boys Town, 1975-1977.* Boys Town, NE: Father Flanagan's Boys' Home.

Phillips, E. L., Phillips, E. A., Fixsen, D. L., & Wolf, M. M. (1974). *The Teaching-Family handbook* (2nd ed.). Lawrence. KS: University Press of Kansas.

Phillips, S. D., Burns, B. J., & Edgar, E. R. (2001). Moving assertive community treatment into standard practice. *Psychiatric Services, 52,* 771-779.

Protheroe, N. (1998). *Comprehensive models for school improvement: Finding the right match and making it work.* Arlington, VA: Educational Research Service.

Reiter-Lavery, L. (2004). *Finding great MST therapists: New and improved hiring guidelines.* Paper presented at the Third International MST Conference, MST Services, Charleston, SC.

Rogers, E. M. (1983). *Diffusion of Innovations* (3rd ed.). New York: The Free Press.

Rogers, R. W. (2002). *White paper-The power of realization.* Retrieved from http://www.ddiworld.com/research/publications.asp

Rohrbach, L. A., D'Onofrio, C. N., Backer, T. E., & Montgomery, S. B. (1996). Diffusion of school-based substance abuse prevention programs. *American Behavioral Scientist, 39*(7), 919-934.

Rosenheck, R. A. (2001). Organizational process: A missing link between research and practice. *Psychiatric Services, 52,* 1607-1612.

Salasin, S. E., & Davis, H. R. (1977). Facilitating the utilization of evaluation: A rocky road. In I. Davidoff, M. Guttentag & J. Offutt (Eds.), *Evaluating community mental health services: Principles and practice* (pp. 428-443). Rockville, MD: National Institute of Mental Health, The Staff College.

Schaffer, E. C., Nesselrodt, P. S., & Stringfield, S. C. (1997). *Impediments to reform: An analysis of destabilizing issues in ten promising programs.* Arlington, VA: Educational Research Service.

Schoenwald, S. J., & Hoagwood, K. (2001). Effectiveness, transportability, and dissemination of interventions: What matters when? *Psychiatric Services, 52,* 1190-1197.

Schoenwald, S. K. (1997). *Rationale for revisions of Medicaid standards for home-based, therapeutic child care, and clinical day programming.* Technical Report prepared for the South Carolina Department of Health and Human Services, Columbia, SC.

Schoenwald, S. K., Brown, T. L., & Henggeler, S. W. (2000). Inside multisystemic therapy: Therapist, supervisory, and program practices. *Journal of Emotional and Behavioral Disorders, 8*(2), 113-127.

Schoenwald, S. K., Sheidow, A. J., & Letourneau, E. J. (2004). Toward effective quality assurance in evidence-based practice: Links between expert consultation, therapist fidelity, and child outcomes. *Journal of Clinical Child and Adolescent Psychology, 33*(1), 94-104.

Schoenwald, S. K., Sheidow, A. J., Letourneau, E. J., & Liao, J. G. (2003). Transportability of multisystemic therapy: Evidence for multilevel influences. *Mental Health Services Research, 5*(4), 223-239.

Schofield, J. (2004). A model of learned implementation. *Public Administration, 82*(2), 283-308.

Schofield, M. J., Edwards, K., & Pearce, R. (1997). Effectiveness of two strategies for dissemination of sun-protection policy in New South Wales primary and secondary schools. *Australian and New Zealand Journal of Public Health, 21*(7), 743.

Showers, B., & Joyce, B. (1996). The evolution of peer coaching. *Educational Leadership, 53*(6).

Slavin, R. E., & Madden, N. A. (1999). *Disseminating Success for All: Lessons for policy and practice* (No. 30). Baltimore: Center for Research on the Education of Students Placed at Risk (CRESPAR) Johns Hopkins University.

Slavin, R. E., & Madden, N. A. (2006). *Success for All, summary of research on achievement outcomes.* Baltimore: Center for Data-Driven Reform in Education (CDDRE), Johns Hopkins University.

Smart, D. A., Blase, K. B., Smart, D. I., Graham, K., Collins, S.R., Daly, P. B., et al. (1979). *The Teaching-Family consultant's handbook* (2nd ed.). Boys Town, NE: Father Flanagan's Boys' Home.

Solomon, D., Battistich, V., Watson, M., Schaps, E., & Lewis, C. (2000). A six-district study of educational change: Direct and mediated effects of the Child Development Project. *Social Psychology of Education, 4,* 3-51.

Sparks, D. (2004). Focusing staff development on improving the learning of all students. In G. Cawelti (Ed.), *Handbook of Research on Improving Student Achievement.* Arlington, VA: Educational Research Service.

Spouse, J. (2001). Bridging theory and practice in the supervisory relationship: A sociocultural perspective. *Journal of Advanced Nursing, 33*(4), 512-522.

Sugai, G., & Horner, R. H. (2002). The evolution of discipline practices: School-wide Positive Behavior Supports. *Child & Family Behavior Therapy 24*(1/2), 23-50.

Taylor, L., Nelson, P., & Adelman, H. (1999). Scaling-up reforms across a school district. *Reading and Writing Quarterly, 15*(4), 303-325.

Unger, J. P., Macq, J., Bredo, F., & Boelaert, M. (2000). Through Mintzberg's glasses: A fresh look at the organization of ministries of health. *Bulletin of the World Health Organization, 78*(8), 1005-1014.

Waltz, J., Addis, M. E., Koerner, K., & Jacobson, N. S. (1993). Testing the integrity of a psychotherapy protocol: Assessment of adherence and competence. *Journal of Consulting and Clinical Psychology, 61*(4), 620-630.

Washington State Institute for Public Policy. (2002). *Washington state's implementation of functional family therapy for juvenile offenders: Preliminary findings* (No. 02-08-1201). Olympia, WA: Author.

Westphal, J. D., Gulati, R., & Shortell, S. M. (1997). Customization or conformity? An institutional and network perspective on the content and consequences of TQM adoption. *Administrative Science Quarterly, 42*(2), 366-394.

Williams, W. (1975). Implementation analysis and assessment. *Policy Analysis, 1*, 531-566.

Wineman, J. H., & Fixsen, D. L. (1979). *The professional evaluator's handbook.* Boys Town, NE: Father Flanagan's Boys' Home.

Winter, S. G., & Szulanski, G. (2001). Replication as strategy. *Organization Science, 12*(6), 730-743.

Yeaton, W. H., & Sechrest, L. (1981). Critical dimensions in the choice and maintenance of successful treatments: Strength, integrity, and effectiveness. *Journal of Consulting & Clinical Psychology, 49*, 156-167.

Zins, J. E., & Illback, R. J. (1995). Consulting to facilitate planned organizational change in schools. *Journal of Educational and Psychological Consultation, 6*(3), 237-245.

Appendix A

Identifying and Implementing Educational Practices Supported by Rigorous Evidence: A User Friendly Guide

Prepared for the:
Institute of Education Sciences
Grover J. Whitehurst, Director

by the Coalition for
Evidence-Based Policy

U.S. Department of Education
Institute of Education Sciences
National Center for Education Evaluation and Regional Assistance
What Works Clearinghouse

This guide seeks to provide assistance to educational practitioners in evaluating whether an educational intervention is backed by rigorous evidence of effectiveness, and in implementing evidence-based interventions in their schools or classrooms. By *intervention*, we mean an educational practice, strategy, curriculum, or program. The guide is organized in four parts:

I.   A description of the randomized controlled trial, and why it is a critical factor in establishing "strong" evidence of an intervention's effectiveness

II. How to evaluate whether an intervention is backed by "strong" evidence of effectiveness

III. How to evaluate whether an intervention is backed by "possible" evidence of effectiveness

IV. Important factors to consider when implementing an evidence-based intervention in your schools or classrooms.

I. The randomized controlled trial: What it is, and why it is a critical factor in establishing "strong" evidence of an intervention's effectiveness.

Well-designed and implemented randomized controlled trials are considered the "gold standard" for evaluating an intervention's effectiveness, in fields such as medicine, welfare and employment policy, and psychology.[7] This section discusses what a randomized controlled trial is, and outlines evidence indicating that such trials should play a similar role in education.

A. Definition: Randomized controlled trials are studies
that randomly assign individuals to an intervention group
or to a control group, in order to measure the effects of
the intervention.

For example, suppose you want to test, in a randomized controlled
trial, whether a new math curriculum for third-graders is more
effective than your school's existing math curriculum for third-
graders. You would randomly assign a large number of third-grade
students to either an intervention group, which uses the new curriculum, or to a control group, which uses the existing curriculum.
You would then measure the math achievement of both groups over
time. The difference in math achievement between the two groups
would represent the effect of the new curriculum compared to the
existing curriculum.

In a variation on this basic concept, sometimes individuals are randomly assigned to two or more intervention groups as well as to a
control group, in order to measure the effects of different interventions in one trial. Also, in some trials, entire classrooms, schools,
or school districts—rather than individual students—are randomly
assigned to intervention and control groups.

B. The unique advantage of random assignment: It enables
you to evaluate whether the intervention itself, as opposed
to other factors, causes the observed outcomes.

Specifically, the process of randomly assigning a large number of individuals to either an intervention group or a control group ensures, to
a high degree of confidence, that there are no systematic differences

between the groups in any characteristics (observed and unobserved) except one—namely, the intervention group participates in the intervention, and the control group does not. Therefore—assuming the trial is properly carried out (per the guidelines below)—the resulting difference in outcomes between the intervention and control groups can confidently be attributed to the intervention and not to other factors.

C. There is persuasive evidence that the randomized controlled trial, when properly designed and implemented, is superior to other study designs in measuring an intervention's true effect.

1. "Pre-post" study designs often produce erroneous results.

Definition: A "pre-post" study examines whether participants in an intervention improve or regress during the course of the intervention, and then attributes any such improvement or regression to the intervention.

The problem with this type of study is that, without reference to a control group, it cannot answer whether the participants' improvement or decline would have occurred anyway, even without the intervention. This often leads to erroneous conclusions about the effectiveness of the intervention.

> **Example:** A randomized controlled trial of Even Start—
> a federal program designed to improve the literacy of disad-
> vantaged families—found that the program had no effect on
> improving the school readiness of participating children at
> the 18th-month follow-up. Specifically, there were no signifi-
> cant differences between young children in the program and
> those in the control group on measures of school readiness,
> including the Picture Peabody Vocabulary Test (PPVT) and
> PreSchool Inventory.[8]

*If a pre-post design rather than a randomized design had been used in
this study*, the study would have concluded erroneously that the program was effective in increasing school readiness. This is because *both*
the children in the program and those in the control group showed
improvement in school readiness during the course of the program
(e.g., both groups of children improved substantially in their national percentile ranking on the PPVT). A pre-post study would have
attributed the participants' improvement to the program, whereas,
in fact, it was the result of other factors, as evidenced by the equal
improvement for children in the control group.

> **Example:** A randomized controlled trial of the Summer Training and Education Program—a Labor Department pilot program that provided summer remediation and work experience for disadvantaged teenagers—found that the program's short-term impact on participants' reading ability was positive. Specifically, while the reading ability of the control group members eroded by a full grade level during the first summer of the program, the reading ability of participants in the program eroded by only a half grade level. [9]

If a pre-post design rather than a randomized design had been used in this study, the study would have concluded erroneously that the program was harmful. That is, the study would have found a decline in participants' reading ability and attributed it to the program. In fact, however, the participants' decline in reading ability was the result of other factors—such as the natural erosion of reading ability during the summer vacation months—as evidenced by the even greater decline for members of the control group.

2. The most common "comparison group" study designs (also known as "quasi-experimental" designs) also lead to erroneous conclusions in many cases.

a. Definition: A "comparison group" study compares outcomes for intervention participants with outcomes for a comparison group chosen through methods other than randomization.

The following example illustrates the basic concept of this design. Suppose you want to use a comparison-group study to test whether a new mathematics curriculum is effective. You would compare the math performance of students who participate in the new curriculum ("intervention group") with the performance of a "comparison group" of students, chosen through methods other than randomization, who do not participate in the curriculum. The comparison group might be students in neighboring classrooms or schools that don't use the curriculum, or students in the same grade and socioeconomic status selected from state or national survey data. The difference in math performance between the intervention and comparison groups following the intervention would represent the estimated effect of the curriculum.

Some comparison-group studies use statistical techniques to create a comparison group that is matched with the intervention group in socioeconomic and other characteristics, or to otherwise adjust for differences between the two groups that might lead to inaccurate estimates of the intervention's effect. The goal of such statistical techniques is to simulate a randomized controlled trial.

b. There is persuasive evidence that the most common comparison-group designs produce erroneous conclusions in a sizeable number of cases.

A number of careful investigations have been carried out—in the areas of school dropout prevention,[10] K-3 class-size reduction,[11] and welfare and employment policy[12]—to examine whether and under what circumstances comparison-group designs can replicate the results of randomized controlled trials.[13] These investigations first compare participants in a particular intervention with a control group, selected through randomization, in order to estimate the intervention's impact in a randomized controlled trial. Then the same intervention participants are compared with a comparison group selected through methods other than randomization, in order to estimate the intervention's impact in a comparison-group design. Any systematic difference between the two estimates represents the inaccuracy produced by the comparison-group design.

These investigations have shown that most comparison-group designs in education and other areas produce inaccurate estimates of an intervention's effect. This is because of unobservable differences between the members of the two groups that differentially affect their outcomes. For example, if intervention participants self-select themselves into the intervention group, they may be more motivated to succeed than their control-group counterparts. Their motivation—rather than the intervention—may then lead to their superior outcomes. In a sizeable number of cases, the inaccuracy produced by the comparison-group designs is large enough to result in erroneous overall conclusions about whether the intervention is effective, ineffective, or harmful.

Example from medicine. Over the past 30 years, more than two dozen comparison-group studies have found hormone replacement therapy for postmenopausal women to be effective in reducing the women's risk of coronary heart disease, by about 35-50 percent. But when hormone therapy was finally evaluated in two large-scale randomized controlled trials—medicine's "gold standard"—it was actually found to do the opposite: it *increased* the risk of heart disease, as well as stroke and breast cancer.[14]

Medicine contains many other important examples of interventions whose effect as measured in comparison-group studies was subsequently contradicted by well-designed randomized controlled trials. If randomized controlled trials in these cases had never been carried out and the comparison-group results had been relied on instead, the result would have been needless death or serious illness for millions of people. This is why the Food and Drug Administration and National Institutes of Health generally use the randomized controlled trial as the final arbiter of which medical interventions are effective and which are not.

3. Well-matched comparison-group studies can be valuable in generating hypotheses about "what works," but their results need to be confirmed in randomized controlled trials.

The investigations, discussed above, that compare comparison-group designs with randomized controlled trials generally support the value of comparison-group designs in which the comparison group is *very closely matched* with the intervention group in prior test scores, demographics, time period in which they are studied, and methods used to collect outcome data. In most cases, such well-matched comparison-group designs seem to yield correct overall conclusions in most cases about whether an intervention is effective, ineffective, or harmful. However, their estimates of the size of the intervention's impact are still often inaccurate. As an illustrative example, a well-matched comparison-group study might find that a program to reduce class size raises test scores by 40 percentile points—or, alternatively, by 5 percentile points—when its true effect is 20 percentile points. Such inaccuracies are large enough to lead to incorrect overall judgments about the policy or practical significance of the intervention in a nontrivial number of cases.

As discussed in section III of this guide, we believe that such well-matched studies can play a valuable role in education, as they have in medicine and other fields, in establishing "possible" evidence of an intervention's effectiveness, and thereby generating hypotheses that merit confirmation in randomized controlled trials. But the evidence cautions strongly against using even the most well-matched comparison-group studies as a final arbiter of what is effective and what is not, or as a reliable guide to the strength of the effect.

D. Thus, we believe there are compelling reasons why randomized controlled trials are a critical factor in establishing "strong" evidence of an intervention's effectiveness.

II. How to evaluate whether an intervention is backed by "strong" evidence of effectiveness.

This section discusses how to evaluate whether an intervention is backed by "strong" evidence that it will improve educational outcomes in your schools or classrooms. Specifically, it discusses both the quality and quantity of studies needed to establish such evidence.

A. Quality of evidence needed to establish "strong" evidence of effectiveness: Randomized controlled trials that are well designed and implemented.

As discussed in section I, randomized controlled trials are a critical factor in establishing "strong" evidence of an intervention's effectiveness. Of course, such trials must also be well designed and implemented in order to constitute strong evidence. Below is an outline of key items to look for when reviewing a randomized controlled trial of an educational intervention, to see whether the trial was well designed and implemented. It is meant as a discussion of general principles, rather than as an exhaustive list of the features of such trials.

Key items to look for in the study's description of the intervention and the random assignment process:

1. The study should clearly describe (i) the intervention, including who administered it, who received it, and what it cost; (ii) how the intervention differed from what the control group received; and (iii) the logic of how the intervention is supposed to affect outcomes.

Example. A randomized controlled trial of a one-on-one tutoring program for beginning readers should discuss such items as:

- who conducted the tutoring (e.g., certified teachers, paraprofessionals, or undergraduate volunteers)

- what training they received in how to tutor

- what curriculum they used to tutor, and other key features of the tutoring sessions (e.g., daily 20-minute sessions over a period of six months)

- the age, reading achievement levels, and other relevant characteristics of the tutored students and controls

- the cost of the tutoring intervention per student

- the reading instruction received by the students in the control group (e.g., the school's preexisting reading program)

- the logic by which tutoring is supposed to improve reading outcomes

2. Be alert to any indication that the random assignment process may have been compromised.

For example, did any individuals randomly assigned to the control group subsequently cross over to the intervention group? Or did individuals unhappy with their prospective assignment to either the intervention or control group have an opportunity to delay their entry into the study until another opportunity arose for assignment to their preferred group? Such self-selection of individuals into their preferred groups undermines the random assignment process, and may well lead to inaccurate estimates of the intervention's effects.

Ideally, a study should describe the method of random assignment it used (e.g., coin toss or lottery), and what steps were taken to prevent undermining (e.g., asking an objective third party to administer the random assignment process). In reality, few studies—even well-designed trials—do this. But we recommend that you be alert to any indication that the random assignment process was compromised.

3. The study should provide data showing that there were no systematic differences between the intervention and control groups before the intervention.

As discussed above, the random assignment process ensures, to a high degree of confidence, that there are no systematic differences between the characteristics of the intervention and control groups prior to the intervention. However, in rare cases—particularly in smaller trials—random assignment might by chance produce intervention and control groups that differ systematically in various characteristics (e.g., academic achievement levels, socioeconomic status, ethnic mix). Such differences could lead to inaccurate results. Thus, the study should provide data showing that, before the intervention, the intervention and control groups did not differ systematically in the vast majority of measured characteristics (allowing that, by chance, there might have been some minor differences).

Key items to look for in the study's collection of outcome data:

---

4. The study should use outcome measures that are "valid"— i.e., that accurately measure the true outcomes that the intervention is designed to affect. Specifically:

- To test academic achievement outcomes (e.g., reading/math skills), a study should use tests whose ability to accurately measure true skill levels is well established (for example, the Woodcock-Johnson Psychoeducational Battery, the Stanford Achievement Test, etc.).

- Wherever possible, a study should use objective, "real-world" measures of the outcomes that the intervention is designed to affect (e.g., for a delinquency prevention program, the students' official suspensions from school).

- If outcomes are measured through interviews or observation, the interviewers/observers preferably should be kept unaware of who is in the intervention and control groups.

Such "blinding" of the interviewers/observers, where possible, helps protect against the possibility that any bias they may have (e.g., as proponents of the intervention) could influence their outcome measurements. Blinding would be appropriate, for example, in a study of a violence prevention program for elementary school students, where an outcome measure is the incidence of hitting on the playground as detected by an adult observer.

- When study participants are asked to "self-report" outcomes, their reports should, if possible, be corroborated by independent and/or objective measures.

For instance, when participants in a substance abuse or violence prevention program are asked to self-report their drug or tobacco use or criminal behavior, they tend to under-report such undesirable behaviors. In some cases, this may lead to inaccurate study results, depending on whether the intervention and control groups under-report by different amounts.

Thus, studies that use such self-reported outcomes should, if possible, corroborate them with other measures (e.g., saliva thiocyanate tests for smoking, official arrest data, third-party observations).

5. The percent of study participants that the study has lost track of when collecting outcome data should be small, and should not differ between the intervention and control groups.

A general guideline is that the study should lose track of fewer than 25 percent of the individuals originally randomized—the fewer lost, the better. This is sometimes referred to as the requirement for "low attrition." (Studies that choose to follow only a representative subsample of the randomized individuals should lose track of less than 25 percent of the subsample.)

Furthermore, the percentage of subjects lost track of should be approximately the same for the intervention and the control groups. This is because differential losses between the two groups can create systematic differences between the two groups, and thereby lead to inaccurate estimates of the intervention's effect. This is sometimes referred to as the requirement for "no differential attrition."

6. The study should collect and report outcome data even for those members of the intervention group who don't participate in or complete the intervention.

This is sometimes referred to as the study's use of an "intention-to-treat" approach, the importance of which is best illustrated with an example.

> **Example.** Consider a randomized controlled trial of a school voucher program, in which students from disadvantaged backgrounds are randomly assigned to an intervention group—whose members are offered vouchers to attend private school—or to a control group that does not receive voucher offers. It's likely that some of the students in the intervention group will not accept their voucher offers and will choose instead to remain in their existing schools. Suppose that, as may well be the case, these students as a group are less motivated to succeed than their counterparts who accept the offer. If the trial then drops the students not accepting the offer from the intervention group, leaving the more motivated students, it would be create a systematic difference between the intervention and control groups—namely, motivation level. Thus the study may well over-estimate the voucher program's effect on educational success, erroneously attributing a superior outcome for the intervention group to the vouchers, when in fact it was due to the difference in motivation.

Therefore, the study should collect outcome data for all of the individuals randomly assigned to the intervention group, *whether they participated in the intervention or not*, and should use all such data in estimating the intervention's effect. The study should also report on how many of the individuals assigned to the intervention group actually participated in the intervention.

7. The study should preferably obtain data on long-term outcomes of the intervention, so that you can judge whether the intervention's effects were sustained over time.

This is important because the effect of many interventions diminishes substantially within 2-3 years after the intervention ends. This has been demonstrated in randomized controlled trials in diverse areas such as early reading, school-based substance abuse prevention, prevention of childhood depression, and welfare-to-work and employment. In most cases, it is the longer-term effect, rather than the immediate effect, that is of greatest practical and policy significance.

> Key items to look for in the study's reporting of results:

8. If the study claims that the intervention improves one or more outcomes, it should report (i) the size of the effect, and (ii) statistical tests showing the effect is unlikely to be due to chance.

Specifically, the study should report the size of the difference in outcomes between the intervention and control groups. It should also report the results of tests showing the difference is "statistically significant" at conventional levels—generally the .05 level. Such a finding means that there is only a 1 in 20 probability that the difference could have occurred by chance if the intervention's true effect is zero.

a. In order to obtain such a finding of statistically significant effects, a study usually needs to have a relatively large sample size.

A rough rule of thumb is that a sample size of at least 300 students (150 in the intervention group and 150 in the control group) is needed to obtain a finding of statistical significance for an intervention that is modestly effective. If schools or classrooms, rather than individual students, are randomized, a minimum sample size of 50 to 60 schools or classrooms (25-30 in the intervention group and 25-30 in the control group) is needed to obtain such a finding. (This rule of thumb assumes that the researchers choose a sample of individuals or schools/classrooms that do not differ widely in initial achievement levels.)[15] If an intervention is highly effective, smaller sample sizes than this may be able to generate a finding of statistical significance.

If the study seeks to examine the intervention's effect on particular subgroups within the overall sample (e.g., Hispanic students), larger sample sizes than those above may be needed to generate a finding of statistical significance for the subgroups.

In general, larger sample sizes are better than smaller sample sizes, because they provide greater confidence that any difference in outcomes between the intervention and control groups is due to the intervention rather than chance.

b. If the study randomizes groups (e.g., schools) rather than individuals, the sample size that the study uses in tests for statistical significance should be the number of groups rather than the number of individuals in those groups.

Occasionally, a study will erroneously use the number of individuals as its sample size, and thus generate false findings of statistical significance.

Example. If a study randomly assigns two schools to an intervention group and two schools to a control group, the sample size that the study should use in tests for statistical significance is just four, regardless of how many hundreds of students are in the schools. (And it is very unlikely that such a small study could obtain a finding of statistical significance.)

---

c. The study should preferably report the size of the intervention's effects in easily understandable, real-world terms (e.g., an improvement in reading skill by two grade levels, a 20 percent reduction in weekly use of illicit drugs, a 20 percent increase in high school graduation rates).

It is important for a study to report the size of the intervention's effects in this way, in addition to whether the effects are statistically significant, so that you (the reader) can judge their educational importance. For example, it is possible that a study with a large sample size could show effects that are statistically significant but so small that they have little practical or policy significance (e.g., a 2-point increase in SAT scores). Unfortunately, some studies report only whether the intervention's effects are statistically significant, and not their magnitude.

Some studies describe the size of the intervention's effects in "standardized effect sizes."[16] A full discussion of this concept is beyond the scope of this guide. We merely comment that standardized effect sizes may not accurately convey the educational importance of an intervention, and, when used, should preferably be translated into understandable, real-world terms like those above.

9. A study's claim that the intervention's effect on a subgroup (e.g., Hispanic students) is different than its effect on the overall population in the study should be treated with caution.

Specifically, we recommend that you look for corroborating evidence of such subgroup effects in other studies before accepting them as valid.

This is because a study will sometimes show different effects for different subgroups just by chance, particularly when the researchers examine a large number of subgroups and/or the subgroups contain a small number of individuals. For example, even if an intervention's true effect is the same on all subgroups, we would expect a study's analysis of 20 subgroups to "demonstrate" a different effect on one of those subgroups just by chance (at conventional levels of statistical significance). Thus, studies that engage in a post-hoc search for different subgroup effects (as some do) will sometimes turn up spurious effects rather than legitimate ones.

> **Example**. In a large randomized controlled trial of aspirin for
> the emergency treatment of heart attacks, aspirin was found to
> be highly effective, resulting in a 23 percent reduction in vascu-
> lar deaths at the one-month follow-up. To illustrate the unre-
> liability of subgroup analyses, these overall results were subdi-
> vided by the patients' astrological birth signs into 12 subgroups.
> Aspirin's effects were similar in most subgroups to those for the
> whole population. However, for two of the subgroups, Libra and
> Gemini, aspirin appeared to have no effect in reducing mortal-
> ity. Clearly it would be wrong to conclude from this analysis that
> heart attack patients born under the astrological signs of Libra
> and Gemini do not benefit from aspirin. [17]

10. The study should report the intervention's effects on all the outcomes that the study measured, not just those for which there is a positive effect.

This is because if a study measures a large number of outcomes, it
may, by chance alone, find positive (and statistically significant) effects on one or a few of those outcomes. Thus, the study should
report the intervention's effects on all measured outcomes so that
you can judge whether the positive effects are the exception or
the pattern.

B. <u>Quantity of evidence</u> needed to establish "strong" evidence of effectiveness.

1. For reasons set out below, we believe "strong" evidence of effectiveness requires:

(i) That the intervention be demonstrated effective, through well-designed randomized controlled trials, in more than one site of implementation.

(ii) That these sites be typical school or community settings, such as public school classrooms taught by regular teachers. Typical settings would not include, for example, specialized classrooms set up and taught by researchers for purposes of the study.

Such a demonstration of effectiveness may require more than one randomized controlled trial of the intervention, or one large trial with more than one implementation site.

2. In addition, the trials should demonstrate the intervention's effectiveness in school settings similar to yours, before you can be confident it will work in your schools and classrooms.

For example, if you are considering implementing an intervention in a large inner-city public school serving primarily minority students, you should look for randomized controlled trials demonstrating the intervention's effectiveness in similar settings. Randomized controlled trials demonstrating its effectiveness in a white, suburban population do not constitute strong evidence that it will work in *your* school.

3. Main reasons why a demonstration of effectiveness in more than one site is needed:

- A single finding of effectiveness can sometimes occur by chance alone. For example, even if all educational interventions tested in randomized controlled trials were ineffective, we would expect 1 in 20 of those trials to "demonstrate" effectiveness by chance alone at conventional levels of statistical significance. Requiring that an intervention be shown effective in two trials (or in two sites of one large trial) reduces the likelihood of such a false positive result to 1 in 400.

- The results of a trial in any one site may be dependent on site-specific factors and thus may not be generalizable to other sites. It is possible, for instance, that an intervention may be highly effective in a school with an unusually talented individual managing the details of implementation, but would not be effective in another school with other individuals managing the detailed implementation.

> **Example.** Two multi-site randomized controlled trials of the Quantum Opportunity Program—a community-based program for disadvantaged high school students providing academic assistance, college and career planning, community service and work experiences, and other services—have found that the program's effects vary greatly among the various program sites. A few sites—including the original program site (Philadelphia)—produced sizeable effects on participants' academic and/or career outcomes, whereas many sites had little or no effect on the same outcomes.[18] Thus, the program's effects appear to be highly dependent on site-specific factors, and it is not clear that its success can be widely replicated.

4. Pharmaceutical medicine provides an important precedent for the concept that "strong" evidence requires a showing of effectiveness in more than one instance.

Specifically, the Food and Drug Administration (FDA) usually requires that a new pharmaceutical drug or medical device be shown effective in more than one randomized controlled trial before the FDA will grant it a license to be marketed. The FDA's reasons for this policy are similar to those discussed above.[19]

III. How to evaluate whether an intervention is backed by "possible" evidence of effectiveness.

Because well-designed and implemented randomized controlled trials are not very common in education, the evidence supporting an intervention frequently falls short of the above criteria for "strong" evidence of effectiveness in one or more respects. For example, the supporting evidence may consist of:

- Only nonrandomized studies

- Only one well-designed randomized controlled trial showing the intervention's effectiveness at a single site

- Randomized controlled trials whose design and implementation contain one or more flaws noted above (e.g., high attrition)

- Randomized controlled trials showing the intervention's effectiveness as implemented by researchers in a laboratory-like setting, rather than in a typical school or community setting

- Randomized controlled trials showing the intervention's effectiveness for students with different academic skills and socioeconomic backgrounds than the students in your schools or classrooms.

Whether an intervention not supported by "strong" evidence is nevertheless supported by "possible" evidence of effectiveness (as opposed to *no* meaningful evidence of effectiveness) is a judgment call that depends, for example, on the extent of the flaws in the randomized controlled trials of the intervention and the quality of any nonrandomized studies that have been done. While this guide cannot foresee and provide advice on all possible scenarios of evidence, it offers in this section a few factors to consider in evaluating whether an intervention not supported by "strong" evidence is nevertheless supported by "possible" evidence.

A. Circumstances in which a comparison-group study can constitute "possible" evidence of effectiveness:

1. The study's intervention and comparison groups should be very closely matched in academic achievement levels, demographics, and other characteristics prior to the intervention.

The investigations, discussed in section I, that compare comparison-group designs with randomized controlled trials, generally support the value of comparison-group designs in which the comparison group is *very closely matched* with the intervention group. In the context of education studies, the two groups should be matched closely in characteristics including:

- Prior test scores and other measures of academic achievement (preferably, the same measures that the study will use to evaluate outcomes for the two groups)

- Demographic characteristics, such as age, sex, ethnicity, poverty level, parents' educational attainment, and single or two-parent family background

- Time period in which the two groups are studied (e.g., the two groups are children entering kindergarten in the same year as opposed to sequential years)

- Methods used to collect outcome data (e.g., the same test of reading skills administered in the same way to both groups)

These investigations have also found that when the intervention and comparison groups differ in such characteristics, the study is unlikely to generate accurate results, even when statistical techniques are then used to adjust for these differences in estimating the intervention's effects.

2. The comparison group should not be comprised of individuals who had the option to participate in the intervention but declined.

This is because individuals choosing not to participate in an intervention may differ systematically in their level of motivation and other important characteristics from the individuals who do choose to participate. The difference in motivation (or other characteristics) may itself lead to different outcomes for the two groups, and thus contaminate the study's estimates of the intervention's effects.

Therefore, the comparison group should be comprised of individuals who did not have the option to participate in the intervention, rather than individuals who had the option but declined.

3. The study should preferably choose the intervention/ comparison groups and outcome measures "prospectively"– that is, before the intervention is administered.

This is because if the groups and outcomes measures are chosen by the researchers *after* the intervention is administered ("retrospectively"), the researchers may consciously or unconsciously select groups and outcome measures so as to generate their desired results. Furthermore, it is often difficult or impossible for the reader of the study to determine whether the researchers did so.

Prospective comparison-group studies are, like randomized controlled trials, much less susceptible to this problem. In the words of the director of drug evaluation for the Food and Drug Administration, "The great thing about a [randomized controlled trial or prospective comparison-group study] is that, within limits, you don't have to believe anybody or trust anybody. The planning for [the study] is prospective; they've written the protocol before they've done the study, and any deviation that you introduce later is completely visible." By contrast, in a retrospective study, "you always wonder how many ways they cut the data. It's very hard to be reassured, because there are no rules for doing it."[20]

4. The study should meet the guidelines set out in section II for a well-designed randomized controlled trial (other than guideline 2 concerning the random-assignment process).

That is, the study should use valid outcome measures, have low attrition, report tests for statistical significance, and so on.

B. Studies that do *not* meet the threshold for "possible" evidence of effectiveness:

1. Pre-post studies, which often produce erroneous results, as discussed in section I.

2. Comparison-group studies in which the intervention and comparison groups are not well matched.

As discussed in section I, such studies also produce erroneous results in many cases, even when statistical techniques are used to adjust for differences between the two groups.

> **Example.** As reported in *Education Week*, several comparison-group studies have been carried out to evaluate the effects of "high-stakes testing"—i.e., state-level policies in which student test scores are used to determine various consequences, such as whether the students graduate or are promoted to the next grade, whether their teachers are awarded bonuses, or whether their school is taken over by the state. These studies compare changes in test scores and dropout rates for students in states with high-stakes testing (the intervention group) to those for students in other states (the comparison groups). Because students in different states differ in many characteristics, such as demographics and initial levels of academic achievement, it is unlikely that these studies provide accurate measures of the effects of high-stakes testing. It is not surprising that these studies reach differing conclusions about the effects of such testing.[21]

3. "Meta-analyses" that combine the results of individual studies that do not themselves meet the threshold for "possible" evidence.

Meta-analysis is a quantitative technique for combining the results of individual studies, a full discussion of which is beyond the scope of this guide. We merely note that when meta-analysis is used to combine studies that themselves may generate erroneous results—such as randomized controlled trials with significant flaws, poorly-matched comparison group studies, and pre-post studies—it will often produce erroneous results as well.

> **Example.** A meta-analysis combining the results of many non-randomized studies of hormone replacement therapy found that such therapy significantly lowered the risk of coronary heart disease.[22] But, as noted earlier, when hormone therapy was subsequently evaluated in two large-scale randomized controlled trials, it was actually found to do the opposite—namely, it increased the risk of coronary disease. The meta-analysis merely reflected the inaccurate results of the individual studies, producing more precise, but still erroneous, estimates of the therapy's effect.

IV. Important factors to consider when implementing an evidence-based intervention in your schools or classrooms.

A. Whether an evidence-based intervention will have a positive effect in your schools or classrooms may depend critically on your adhering closely to the details of its implementation.

The importance of adhering to the details of an evidence-based intervention when implementing it in your schools or classrooms is often not fully appreciated. Details of implementation can sometimes make a major difference in the intervention's effects, as the following examples illustrate.

Example. The Tennessee Class-Size Experiment—a large, multi-site randomized controlled trial involving 12,000 students—showed that a state program that significantly reduced class size for public school students in grades K-3 had positive effects on educational outcomes. For example, the average student in the small classes scored higher on the Stanford Achievement Test in reading and math than about 60 percent of the students in the regular-sized classes, and this effect diminished only slightly at the fifth-grade follow-up.[23]

Based largely on these results, in 1996 the state of California launched a much larger, statewide class-size reduction effort for students in grades K-3. But to implement this effort, California schools hired 25,000 new K-3 teachers, many with low qualifications. Thus the proportion of fully-credentialed K-3 teachers fell in most California schools, with the largest drop (16 percent) occurring in the schools serving the lowest-income students. By contrast, all the teachers in the Tennessee study were fully qualified. This difference in implementation may account for the fact that, according to preliminary comparison-group data, class-size reduction in California may not be having as large an impact as in Tennessee.[24]

Example. Three well-designed randomized controlled trials have established the effectiveness of the Nurse-Family Partnership—a nurse visitation program provided to low-income, mostly single women during pregnancy and their children's infancy. One of these studies included a 15-year follow-up, which found that the program reduced the children's arrests, convictions, number of sexual partners, and alcohol use by 50-80 percent.[25]

Fidelity of implementation appears to be extremely important for this program. Specifically, one of the randomized controlled trials of the program showed that when the home visits are carried out by paraprofessionals rather than nurses—holding all other details the same—the program is only marginally effective.

Furthermore, a number of other home visitation programs for low-income families, designed for different purposes and using different protocols, have been shown in randomized controlled trials to be ineffective.[26]

B. When implementing an evidence-based intervention, it may be important to collect outcome data to check whether its effects in your schools differ greatly from what the evidence predicts.

Collecting outcome data is important because it is always possible that slight differences in implementation or setting between your schools or classrooms and those in the studies could lead to substantially different outcomes. So, for example, if you implement an evidence-based reading program in a particular group of schools or classrooms, you may wish to identify a comparison group of schools or classrooms, roughly matched in reading skills and demographic characteristics, that is not using the program. Tracking reading test scores for the two groups over time, while perhaps not fully meeting the guidelines for "possible" evidence described above, may still give you a sense of whether the program is having effects that are markedly different from what the evidence predicts.

References

[7] See, for example, the Food and Drug Administration's standard for assessing the effectiveness of pharmaceutical drugs and medical devices, at 21 C.F.R. §314.126. See also, "The Urgent Need to Improve Health Care Quality," Consensus statement of the Institute of Medicine National Roundtable on Health Care Quality, *Journal of the American Medical Association*, vol. 280, no. 11, September 16, 1998, p. 1003; and Gary Burtless, "The Case for Randomized Field Trials in Economic and Policy Research," *Journal of Economic Perspectives*, vol. 9, no. 2, spring 1995, pp. 63-84.

[8] Robert G. St. Pierre et. al., "Improving Family Literacy: Findings From the National Even Start Evaluation," Abt Associates, September 1996.

[9] Jean Baldwin Grossman, "Evaluating Social Policies: Principles and U.S. Experience," *The World Bank Research Observer*, vol. 9, no. 2, July 1994, pp. 159-181.

[10] Roberto Agodini and Mark Dynarski, "Are Experiments the Only Option? A Look at Dropout Prevention Programs," Mathematica Policy Research, Inc., August 2001, at http://www.mathematica-mpr.com/PDFs/redirect. asp?strSite=experonly.pdf.

[11] Elizabeth Ty Wilde and Rob Hollister, "How Close Is Close Enough? Testing Nonexperimental Estimates of Impact against Experimental Estimates of Impact with Education Test Scores as Outcomes," Institute for Research on Poverty Discussion paper, no. 1242-02, 2002, at http://www.ssc. wisc.edu/irp/.

[12]Howard S. Bloom et. al., "Can Nonexperimental Comparison Group
   Methods Match the Findings from a Random Assignment Evaluation
   of Mandatory Welfare-to-Work Programs?" MDRC Working Paper
   on Research Methodology, June 2002, at http://www.mdrc.org/
   ResearchMethodologyPprs.htm. James J. Heckman, Hidehiko Ichimura,
   and Petra E. Todd, "Matching As An Econometric Evaluation Estimator:
   Evidence from Evaluating a Job Training Programme," *Review of Economic
   Studies*, vol. 64, no. 4, 1997, pp. 605-654. Daniel Friedlander and
   Philip K. Robins, "Evaluating Program Evaluations: New Evidence on
   Commonly Used Nonexperimental Methods," *American Economic Review*,
   vol. 85, no. 4, September 1995, pp. 923-937; Thomas Fraker and Rebecca
   Maynard, "The Adequacy of Comparison Group Designs for Evaluations
   of Employment-Related Programs," *Journal of Human Resources*, vol. 22,
   no. 2, spring 1987, pp. 194-227; Robert J. LaLonde, "Evaluating the
   Econometric Evaluations of Training Programs With Experimental Data,"
   American Economic Review, vol. 176, no. 4, September 1986, pp. 604-620.

[13] This literature, including the studies listed in the three preceding endnotes,
   is systematically reviewed in Steve Glazerman, Dan M. Levy, and
   David Myers, "Nonexperimental Replications of Social Experiments:
   A Systematic Review," Mathematica Policy Research discussion paper,
   no. 8813-300, September 2002. The portion of this review addressing
   labor market interventions is published in "Nonexperimental versus
   Experimental Estimates of Earnings Impact," *The American Annals of
   Political and Social Science,* vol. 589, September 2003.

[14] J.E. Manson et. al, "Estrogen Plus Progestin and the Risk of Coronary Heart
   Disease," *New England Journal of Medicine*, August 7, 2003, vol. 349,
   no. 6, pp. 519-522. *International Position Paper on Women's Health and
   Menopause: A Comprehensive Approach*, National Heart, Lung, and Blood
   Institute of the National Institutes of Health, and Giovanni Lorenzini
   Medical Science Foundation, NIH Publication No. 02-3284, July 2002,
   pp. 159-160. Stephen MacMahon and Rory Collins, "Reliable Assessment
   of the Effects of Treatment on Mortality and Major Morbidity, II:
   Observational Studies," *The Lancet*, vol. 357, February 10, 2001, p. 458.
   Sylvia Wassertheil-Smoller et. al., "Effect of Estrogen Plus Progestin on
   Stroke in Postmenopausal Women—The Women's Health Initiative: A
   Randomized Controlled Trial, *Journal of the American Medical Association*,
   May 28, 2003, vol. 289, no. 20, pp. 2673-2684.

[15] Howard S. Bloom, "Sample Design for an Evaluation of the Reading First Program," an MDRC paper prepared for the U.S. Department of Education, March 14, 2003. Robert E. Slavin, "Practical Research Designs for Randomized Evaluations of Large-Scale Educational Interventions: Seven Desiderata," paper presented at the annual meeting of the American Educational Research Association, Chicago, April, 2003.

[16] The "standardized effect size" is calculated as the difference in the mean outcome between the treatment and control groups, divided by the pooled standard deviation.

[17] Rory Collins and Stephen MacMahon, "Reliable Assessment of the Effects of Treatment on Mortality and Major Morbidity, I: Clinical Trials," *The Lancet*, vol. 357, February 3, 2001, p. 375.

[18] Robinson G. Hollister, "The Growth of After-School Programs and Their Impact," paper commissioned by the Brookings Institution's Roundtable on Children, February 2003, at http://www.brook.edu/dybdocroot/views/papers/sawhill/20030225.pdf. Myles Maxfield, Allen Schirm, and Nuria Rodriguez-Planas, "The Quantum Opportunity Program Demonstration: Implementation and Short-Term Impacts," Mathematica Policy Research (no. 8279-093), August 2003.

[19] *Guidance for Industry: Providing Clinical Evidence of Effectiveness for Human Drugs and Biological Products*, Food and Drug Administration, May 1998, pp. 2-5

[20] Robert J. Temple, Director of the Office of Medical Policy, Center for Drug Evaluation and Research, Food and Drug Administration, quoted in Gary Taubes, "Epidemiology Faces Its Limits," *Science*, vol. 269, issue 5221, p. 169.

[21] Debra Viadero, "Researchers Debate Impact of Tests," *Education Week*, vol. 22, no. 21, February 5, 2003, page 1.

[22] E. Barrett-Connor and D. Grady, "Hormone Replacement Therapy, Heart Disease, and Other Considerations," *Annual Review of Public Health*, vol. 19, 1998, pp. 55-72.

[23] Frederick Mosteller, Richard J. Light, and Jason A. Sachs, op. cit., no. 3.

[24] Brian Stecher et. all, "Class-Size Reduction in California: A Story of Hope, Promise, and Unintended Consequences," *Phi Delta Kappan*, Vol. 82, Iss. 9, May 2001, pp. 670-674.

[25] David L. Olds et. al., "Long-term Effects of Nurse Home Visitation on Children's Criminal and Antisocial Behavior: 15-Year Followup of a Randomized Controlled Trial," *Journal of the American Medical Association*, vol. 280, no. 14, October 14, 1998, pp. 1238-1244. David L. Olds et. al., "Long-term Effects of Home Visitation on Maternal Life Course and Child Abuse and Neglect: 15-Year Follow-up of a Randomized Trial," *Journal of the American Medical Association*, vol. 278, no. 8, pp. 637-643. David L. Olds et. al, "Home Visiting By Paraprofessionals and By Nurses: A Randomized, Controlled Trial," *Pediatrics*, vol. 110, no. 3, September 2002, pp. 486-496. Harriet Kitzman et. al., "Effect of Prenatal and Infancy Home Visitation by Nurses on Pregnancy Outcomes, Childhood Injuries, and Repeated Childbearing," *Journal of the American Medical Association*, vol. 278, no. 8, August 27, 1997, pp. 644-652.

[26] For example, see Robert G. St. Pierre et. al., op. cit., no. 8; Karen McCurdy, "Can Home Visitation Enhance Maternal Social Support?" *American Journal of Community Psychology*, vol. 29, no. 1, 2001, pp. 97-112.

Appendix B

Evaluating the Quality of Evidence From Correlational Research for Evidence-Based Practice

Bruce Thompson, Karen E. Diamond, Robin McWilliam, Patricia Snyder, and Scott W. Snyder

ABSTRACT: Only true experiments offer definitive evidence for causal inferences, but not all educational interventions are readily amenable to experiments. Correlational evidence can at least tentatively inform evidence-based practice when sophisticated causal modeling or exclusion methods are employed. Correlational evidence is most informative when exemplary practices are followed as regards (a) measurement, (b) quantifying effects, (c) avoiding common analysis errors, and (d) using confidence intervals to portray the range of possible effects and the precisions of the effect estimates.

In their recent article in the *Educational Researcher*, Feuer, Towne, and Shavelson (2002) asked, What are the most effective means of stimulating more and better scientific educational research?… [T]he *primary emphasis* [italics added] should be on nurturing and reinforcing a scientific culture of educational research. (p. 4)

They defined scientific culture as "a set of norm and practices and an ethos of honesty, openness, and continuous reflection, *including how research quality is judged*" (Feuer, Towne, & Shavelson, 2002, p. 4, italics added). Recent movements to emphasize evidence-based practice in medicine (see Sackett, Straus, Richardson, Rosenberg, & Haynes, 2000), psychology (see Chambless, 1998), and education (Mosteller & Boruch, 2002; Shavelson & Towne, 2002) also reflect the necessity for standards with which to evaluate research evidence, including evidence from correlational designs.

What Is Correlational Evidence?

Correlational studies can be defined in various ways. In one sense, *all* analyses are correlational (Cohen, 1968; Knapp, 1978; Thompson, 2000a). Because all conventional parametric analyses (e.g., *t*-tests, ANOVA, ANCOVA) are correlational (Bagozzi, Fornell, & Larcker, 1981), in a sense every quantitative study yields correlational evidence. Distinguishing evidence types by focusing on the analysis is not useful because under such a broad definition, all evidence would fall under this single umbrella. Furthermore, a given analysis (e.g., multiple regression) can be correctly employed to analyze data from numerous designs (e.g., a true experiment, a comparative design). A more useful distinction regarding types of evidence focuses not on the analysis, but on the *design* of the study yielding the evidence.

Correlational studies are *quantitative, multisubject designs in which participants have not been randomly assigned to treatment conditions.* Analytic methods commonly (but not exclusively) applied with such designs are multiple regression analysis, canonical correlation analysis, hierarchical linear modeling, and structural equation modeling.

For example, as defined here, a correlational study might investigate differential achievement levels of students enrolled in classes of different sizes, where the students were not randomly assigned to classes of given sizes. Or researchers might collect data regarding the frequency with which teachers praise students, to examine relationships of these behaviors with students' selfconcepts and school attendance.

How Can Correlational Evidence Inform Practice?

Definitive causal conclusions in quantitative research can only be reached on the basis of true randomized trials. That is why it is so important for educational researchers to conduct more true experiments. Historically, randomization has been too infrequently invoked within the social sciences (Ludbrook & Dudley, 1998). However, for various reasons, evidence from types of research not involving randomized clinical trials is also relevant to evidence-based practice.

It is crucial to match research questions and research designs, and some questions are best addressed with nonexperimental designs. For example, questions involving school or classroom culture may require qualitative methods, and questions involving the intensive study of learning dynamics of individual children may require single-subject studies. Even when group quantitative methods are appropriate, randomized experiments may not be ideal if the immature state of knowledge on a given issue does not yet justify the expense of such trials. And in some cases clinical trials may raise ethical questions regarding denial of needed services to control group participants. Not all questions can be addressed with clinical trials, and unduly widespread use of clinical trials would also be undesirable because cross-contamination of effects across children involved in multiple experiments would then compromise all results.

Correlational designs do not provide the best evidence regarding causal mechanisms. Nevertheless, in at least two ways correlational evidence can be used to inform causal inferences and thus evidence-based practice. The first approach is *statistically based*, and involves statistically testing rival alternative causal models, even though the design is correlational. The second method is *logic based* and invokes logic and theory with nonexperimental data in an attempt to rule out all reasonable alternative explanations in support of making a single plausible causal inference.

Statistical Testing of Rival Causal Models

The analytic methods that today we call structural equation modeling (SEM; or covariance structure analysis) originated in the work of Karl Jöreskog (e.g., 1969, 1970, 1971, 1978), and the computer program, LISREL (i.e., analysis of *LI*near *S*tructural *REL*ationships) developed by Jöreskog and his colleagues (e.g., Jöreskog & Sörbom, 1989). These methods as originated in the 1960s and 1970s were then often called *causal modeling*, which hints at the potential of SEM to inform causal inferences.

SEM incorporates factor (or measurement) models, building on the factor analytic methods proposed by Spearman (1904), and a structural model linking these latent constructs, building on the path analytic methods proposed by Wright (1921, 1934). Within the structural model, analysts may test whether (a) two latent constructs (X and Y) covary or are correlated, (b) X causes Y, (c) Y causes X, or (d) X and Y reciprocally cause each other.

The appeal of SEM is that rival models can, and indeed should, be tested (see Thompson, 2000b). If only one of these four models fits the data (e.g., a model specifying that X causes Y), then there is at least some evidence bearing on the existence of a causal relationship.

For example, data reported by Bagozzi (1980) have been used in several reports to illustrate this application (see Jöreskog & Sörbom, 1989, pp. 151–156, and Thompson, 1998b, pp. 37–39). Bagozzi's study investigated the job satisfaction and job performance of 122 workers. For these data, it appeared that a model positing that job performance leads to job satisfaction better fit the data than did models positing that job satisfaction leads to job performance or that satisfaction and performance are reciprocally related.

Logically-Based Exclusion Methods

In some cases when true experiments are not performed, and even when structural modeling is not used, we still may be able to reach causal inferences with some degree of confidence. The capacity for extracting causal information from nonexperimental designs (e.g., intervention studies not invoking random assignment to groups) turns on our capacity to evaluate whether all relevant preintervention differences and design validity threats can be excluded (i.e., deemed essentially irrelevant).

Definitive causal conclusions in quantitative research can only be reached on the basis of true randomized trials.

For example, let's say two intact (i.e., not randomly assigned) groups of special education students were taught reading with two different curricula. We want to make some causal interpretation of the postintervention reading differences in the two conditions. We might investigate preintervention differences in the students on everything that we consider as being even potentially relevant (e.g., preintervention reading scores, socioeconomic status). We might also try to confirm that there were no meaningful extraneous contaminants of treatment influences (e.g., teachers had similar backgrounds in both conditions, curricula were implemented with fidelity). If we can rule out all such problems, we may have at least some plausible evidence that one curriculum is superior to the other curriculum, even though we have not performed a true experiment, and we have not statistically tested rival causal models.

The challenge to such efforts is that we may not be certain exactly which preintervention differences or what design validity threats are relevant in a given study. The beauty of true experiments is that the law of large numbers creates preintervention group equivalencies on *all* variables, even variables that we do not realize are essential to control.

But exclusion methods may be necessary in an environment where true experiments can not be used to address every important intervention question. And as our knowledge base grows, we may become more certain regarding which preintervention differences or treatment confounds are most noteworthy.

Limitations of Nonexperimental Research

Both statistical modeling and logical exclusion methods require that models are "correctly specified." That is, the analytic results are sound only to the extent that

- All the correct variables, and only the correct variables, are employed within the tested models.
- The correct dynamics (e.g., mediation, moderation) are specified within the tested models (i.e., the correct analysis is used).

But as Pedhazur (1982) has noted, "The rub, however, is that the true model is seldom, if ever, known" (p. 229). And as Duncan (1975) has noted, "Indeed it would require no elaborate sophistry to show that we will never have the 'right' model in any absolute sense" (p. 101). Thus, both methods must be used cautiously in applying correlational evidence to help inform evidence-based practice. Nevertheless, correlation evidence, like other nonexperimental evidence, is relevant to evidence-based practice.

Purpose of the Present Article

Educational research has sometimes been criticized for being poorly conducted (see Gall, Borg, & Gall, 1996, p. 151). For example, the National Academy of Science evaluated educational research generically and found "methodologically weak research, trivial studies, an infatuation with jargon, and a tendency toward fads with a consequent fragmentation of effort" (Atkinson & Jackson, 1992, p. 20). Nevertheless, even imperfect studies may provide some useful information. Few defects in published studies are sufficiently egregious to warrant total disqualification from any consideration.

A possible exception to this generalization encompasses studies using stepwise methods (Snyder, 1991). As Huberty (1994) noted, "It is quite common to find the use of 'stepwise analyses' reported in empirically based journal articles" (p. 261). Thompson (1995, 2001) explained that stepwise methods (a) do not correctly identify the best subset of predictors, (b) yield results that tend to be nonreplicable, and (c) "are positively satanic in their temptations toward Type I errors" (Cliff, 1987, p. 185), because most computer programs incorrectly compute the degrees of freedom for stepwise analyses. When researchers must select a subset of variables from a larger constellation of choices, the "all-possible-subsets" analyses described by Huberty (1994), and available in SAS, provide reasonable results.

The present article proposes some quality indicators for evaluating correlational research in efforts to inform evidence-based practice. Given the inherent challenges of educational research (Berliner, 2002), most studies are unavoidably imperfect and vary in the quality of the evidence they provide.

The quality indicators proposed are not new. But they may be insufficiently honored in contemporary analytic practice. For example, various effect size statistics have been proposed for decades (Huberty, 2002), but studies have shown effect sizes to be reported in less than half the published articles in various journals and various disciplines (see Thompson, 1999b; Vacha-Haase, Nilsson, Reetz, Lance, &, Thompson, 2000). Similarly, confidence intervals have been recommended for years (see Chandler, 1957), but empirical studies suggest that intervals are infrequently reported in published social science research (Kieffer, Reese, & Thompson, 2001).

The quality indicators presented are grouped into four sets: (a) measurement; (b) practical and clinical significance; (c) avoidance of some common analytic mistakes; and (d) confidence intervals for score reliability coefficients, statistics, and effect sizes. These are not the only indicator categories that might be identified, but the present categories will serve reasonably well to distinguish some recognizable features of correlational inquiry. Where space limitations preclude in-depth exploration of concerns, helpful references providing further elaboration are routinely provided.

Measurement

The quality of the evidence informing practice is inherently limited by the psychometric integrity of the data being analyzed in a given study. Classically, measurement concerns are conceptualized as involving two primary considerations: score reliability and score validity. However, some modern measurement theories actually present a unified view of these concerns, such that reliability and validity issues are blended (Brennan, 2001).

Reliability can be conceptualized as addressing the question, "Do the scores measure anything?" (i.e., are nonrandom), and *validity* addresses the question, "Do the scores measure only the correct something that they are supposed to measure?" (Thompson, 2003). In this classical measurement view, reliability is a necessary but insufficient condition for validity.

Researchers have traditionally recognized that score validity is not immutable within a given measure; the same measure may yield scores valid for some purposes and respondents, and invalid for other inferences or respondents (Schmidt & Hunter, 1977). Lately, more researchers have come to realize in a similar vein that a given test also is not immutably reliable. As Wilkinson and the American Psychological Association (APA) Task Force on Statistical Inference (1999) recently emphasized:

> It is important to remember that a test is not reliable or unreliable.... Thus, authors should provide reliability coefficients of the scores for the data being analyzed even when the focus of their research is not psychometric. (p. 596)

Unfortunately, recent empirical studies of published research reports indicate that the vast preponderance of articles do not even mention reliability, much less report reliability for the data actually being analyzed (Vacha-Haase, Henson, & Caruso, 2002). These practices may originate in misconceptions that tests are reliable, and that once reliability has been established in a given sample, further concerns are moot (Thompson, 2003; Vacha-Haase, 1998).

A problematic practice is to "induct" the reliability coefficient from a prior study or a test manual (Vacha-Haase et al., 2002). Unfortunately, this induction of prior reliability coefficients turns on the premises that (a) the samples are comparable in their compositions and (b) the scores are roughly equivalent in their standard deviations across studies (Crocker & Algina, 1986, p. 144). Sadly, empirical studies suggest that such inductions are almost never explicitly justified and often are wildly inappropriate (Vacha-Haase, Kogan, &, Thompson, 2000; Whittington, 1998). It is unacceptable to induct the score reliability coefficients from prior studies or test manuals if there is no *explicit* evidence presented that the sample compositions and the standard deviations from the prior study and a current study are *both* reasonably comparable.

Recent empirical studies of published research reports indicate that the vast preponderance of articles do not even mention reliability, much less report reliability for the data actually being analyzed.

Quality Indicators:

- Score reliability coefficients are reported for all measured variables, based on induction from a prior study or test manual, with explicit and reasonable justifications as regards comparabilities of (a) sample compositions and (b) score dispersions.
- Score reliability coefficients are reported for all measured variables based on analysis of the data in hand in the particular study.
- Evidence is inducted, with explicit rationale, from a prior study or test manual that suggests scores are valid for the inferences being made in the study.

- Score validity is empirically evaluated based on data generated within the study.
- The influences of score reliability and validity on study interpretations are explicitly considered in reasonable detail.

Practical and Clinical Significance

Statistical significance estimates the probability, p, of sample results, given the sample size, and assuming the sample came from a population exactly described by the null hypothesis (Cohen, 1994; Thompson, 1996). In disciplines as diverse as wildlife sciences and psychology, the utility of statistical significance has been increasingly questioned in recent years (Anderson, Burnham, & Thompson, 2000; see Harlow, Mulaik, & Steiger, 1997 and Nickerson, 2000 for comprehensive summaries of both sides of the controversy). Indeed, a forthcoming issue of the *Journal of Socio-Economics* (see Thompson, in press-b) will include commentary by several economics Nobel laureates on this issue.

Practical significance evaluates the potential noteworthiness of study results, by quantifying the degree to which sample results diverge from the null hypothesis (Snyder & Lawson, 1993). These quantifications are often referred to generically as "effect sizes." There are literally dozens of effect size statistics (see Kirk, 1996). Many of these myriad choices can be arrayed within the following categories: (a) standardized differences (e.g., Cohen's *d*, Glass's D), (b) "uncorrected" variance-accounted-for (e.g., h2, *R*2), and (c) "corrected" variance-accounted-for (e.g., adjusted *R*2, w2; see Thompson, 2002a). Thompson (in press-a), Kirk (1996), and Snyder and Lawson (1993) provide reviews on the numerous available choices.

Clinical significance evaluates the extent to which intervention recipients no longer meet diagnostic criteria (e.g., learning disability, depression), and, thus, no longer require specialized intervention (Jacobson, Roberts, Berns, & McGlinchey, 1999; Kendall, 1999). Clinical significance is potentially relevant *only* when the outcome variable can be interpreted using accepted diagnostic criteria (e.g., total cholesterol greater than 200 milligrams).

The fifth edition of the APA (2001) *Publication Manual* emphasized that

> It is *almost always necessary* to include some index of effect size or strength of relationship.... The general principle to be followed...is to provide the reader not only with information about statistical significance but also with enough information to assess the magnitude of the observed effect or relationship. (pp. 25–26, emphasis added)

The manual also describes failure to report effect sizes as "a defect" (p. 5). But the editors of 23 journals have gone beyond the APA *Publication Manual* and have published author guidelines requiring effect size reporting (Fidler, 2002).

Jacob Cohen, in his various books on power analysis, provided benchmarks for effect sizes that he deemed small, medium, and large. He formulated these based on his impressions of the range of effect sizes typical of the social science literature as a whole. He hesitated to provide such benchmarks because he felt that effects ought to be interpreted instead against the criteria of the researcher's values and related effects reported in prior literature. However, he provided these benchmarks of typicality because he felt that researchers would be more likely to report effect sizes if there were some standards for interpreting them, pending the reporting of effect sizes becoming routine within the literature. But "if people interpreted effect sizes [using fixed benchmarks] with the same rigidity that a = .05 has been used in statistical testing, we would merely be being stupid in another metric" (Thompson, 2001, pp. 82–83).

Glass, McGaw, and Smith (1981) argued that "there is no wisdom whatsoever in attempting to associate regions of the effect-size metric with descriptive adjectives such as 'small,' 'moderate,' 'large,' and the like" (p. 104). The only exception to this rule involves groundbreaking inquiry in which little or no previous research has been conducted, in which case Cohen's benchmarks may be useful as a (very) rough guide.

The problem is *not* the use of adjectives such as large or small. The problem is using fixed, generic benchmarks for making these judgments, rather than consulting the effects in related studies.

The results of a single study have meaning primarily as regards what they contribute to a literature, although, of course, the results of a single study sometimes do change thinking about a phenomenon (Thompson, in press-a). The comparison of effects against those reported in related prior studies enables researchers to evaluate the consistency of results across studies. This powerful view of all quantitative research as requiring "meta-analytic thinking" (Cumming & Finch, 2001; Thompson, 2002b) is promoted by interpreting results across studies. Such direct comparisons also alert researchers to inconsistent findings, which may highlight moderator variables or situations in which results vary across different subpopulations.

Common Mistakes

Even today when 23 journals (see McLean & Kaufman, 2000; Snyder, 2000) require effect size reporting, effect size reporting is more the exception than the norm (see Thompson, 1999b; Vacha-Haase, Nilsson et al., 2000). This does make it more difficult to interpret the effects in a given study in direct, explicit comparison with the effect sizes reported in prior studies, because effects must be computed or estimated for prior studies in which authors did not report effect sizes.

Effect sizes should be reported for all primary study outcomes, even when particular results are not statistically significant (Thompson, 2002b). Such reporting facilitates future metaanalytic integration of the study into the corpus of the literature.

Furthermore, some researchers do report, but do not interpret, their effect sizes (Vacha-Haase, Nilsson et al., 2000). Reporting, but not interpreting, effect sizes does not allow effect sizes to inform fully the interpretation of results.

A fundamental, but too common, mistake is failing to identify which effect size is being reported. Because there are so many different effect sizes (see Kirk, 1996), some with different ranges and properties, it is critical to identify reported effect statistics explicitly.

Finally, it is also important to recognize that effect sizes cannot magically escape the limitations or analytic assumptions of given analyses (Olejnik & Algina, 2000). These limitations and assumptions should be considered as part of result interpretation.

Quality Indicators:

- One or more effect size statistics is reported for each study primary outcome, and the effect statistic used is clearly identified.
- Authors interpret study effect sizes for selected practices by directly and explicitly comparing study effects with those reported in related prior studies.
- Authors explicitly consider study design and effect size statistic limitations as part of effect interpretation.

Avoidance of Some Common Macro-Analytic Mistakes

Across the literature a range of analytic errors are seen with some frequency. Some of these errors are unique to a particular method. For example, it is common for researchers to confuse descriptive discriminant analysis with predictive discriminant analysis, or vice versa, and consequently to misinterpret their discriminant analysis results (see Huberty, 1994; Kieffer et al., 2001). Other analytic errors occur generally across analytic choices.

Research evidence better informs practice when these errors are avoided. Here four such common generic, macro-analytic errors are noted. These can occur across two or more, or in some cases, all correlational analytic methods.

Failure to Interpret Structure Coefficients

Throughout the general linear model (GLM), weights are either explicitly (e.g., regression, descriptive discriminant analysis) or implicitly (e.g., *t*-tests, ANOVA) applied to measured variables to estimate the scores on the latent variables that are actually the focus of the analysis (see Thompson, 2000a). These weights are given different names across analyses (e.g., beta weights, factor pattern coefficients, discriminant function coefficients), which has the effect of obfuscating the existence of the GLM.

When researchers obtain noteworthy effects, they commonly (and correctly) consult these weights as part of the process of determining the origins of detected effects. However, these weights are usually *not* correlation coefficients of predictors with outcome variables. In fact, a predictor may have the largest nonzero weight in an analysis even when the predictor is perfectly uncorrelated with the outcome variable (Thompson & Borrello, 1985).

Structure coefficients (i.e., correlations of measured variables with the latent variables actually being analyzed, such as regression ¯ scores) are also usually *essential* to correct interpretation (Courville & Thompson, 2001; Dunlap & Landis, 1998). For example, structure coefficients have been characterized as essential to the correct interpretation of multiple regression analysis (Courville & Thompson), exploratory factor analysis (Gorsuch, 1983, p. 207), confirmatory factor analysis (Graham, Guthrie, &, Thompson, 2003), descriptive discriminant analysis (Huberty, 1994), and canonical correlation analysis (Thompson, 1984).

Quality Indicators:

- GLM weights (e.g., beta weights) are interpreted as reflecting correlations of predictors with outcome variables only in the exceptional case that the weights indeed are correlation coefficients.
- When noteworthy results are detected, and the origins of these effects are investigated, the interpretation includes examination of structure coefficients.

Effect sizes should be reported for all primary study outcomes, even when particular results are not statistically significant.

Converting Intervally Scaled Variables to Nominal Scale

It is not uncommon (Pedhazur, 1982, pp. 452–453) to see researchers convert one or more of their independent or predictor variables into nominal scale in order to run OVA methods (e.g., ANOVA). For example, researchers may take intervally- scaled pretest data (e.g., IQ scores, pretest achievement scores) and characterize participants as either "low" or "high" in learning aptitude.

Such dichotomization (trichotomization, etc.) (a) "throws information away" (i.e., discards score variability; Kerlinger, 1986, p. 558); (b) attenuates reliability of the scores being analyzed; (c) distorts variable distributions; and (d) distorts relationships among variables (Thompson, 1986). The result is analyses that are ecologically less valid.

In her comprehensive Monte Carlo study, Hester (2000) provided considerably more detail on the consequences of such ill-considered analytic choices. The consequences of these conversions are particularly deleterious for building an integrated literature when different researchers use divergent cutoffs (e.g., different sample-specific median splits) to implement the conversions. For example, if researcher Jones dichotomizes pretest IQ data at Jones's sample median of 95, and researcher Smith does so at Smith's sample median of 105, we will never know whether discrepant ANOVA or MANOVA results are (a) an artifact of using different cutpoints to dichotomize, or (b) a failure to replicate results.

Quality Indicator:

- Interval data are not converted to nominal scale, unless such choices are justified on the extraordinary basis of distribution shapes, and the consequences of the conversion are thoughtfully considered as part of result interpretation.

Inappropriate Univariate Methods

Univariate methods (i.e., analyses using a single dependent variable) are quite commonly used in educational research (Kieffer et al., 2001). These methods can be quite appropriate for some studies. However, there are two situations in which univariate methods are inappropriate.

First, *univariate methods are generally inappropriate in the presence of multiple outcomes variables.* The use of univariate methods when a study involves several outcome variables (a) inflates the probability of experimentwise Type I errors, and (b) does not honor the reality that outcome variables can interact with each other to define unique outcomes that are more than their constituent parts (Fish, 1988).

Regarding the second concern, Thompson (1999a) provided a heuristic data set illustrating the importance of these issues. In his example data set, the two means on X and Y did not differ to a statistically significant degree (both ANOVA p values were .774), and furthermore the ANOVA eta^2 effect sizes were both computed to be 0.469%. Thus, the two sets of ANOVA results were not statistically significant, and they both involved extremely small effect sizes. However, a MANOVA/descriptive discriminant analysis (DDA) of the *same data* yielded a pCALCULATED value of .0002, and a multivariate eta^2 of 62.5%!

This means that the Bonferroni correction in the presence of several or many outcome variables is *not* suitable, for two reasons. First, the correction lowers power against Type II error. Second, multiple univariate analyses do not honor the ecological reality that all the variables, including the outcomes, can interact with each other to create unique effects that will only be discovered in a multivariate analysis.

Second, *the use of univariate methods (e.g., ANOVA) post hoc to multivariate tests is inappropriate*, albeit common (Kieffer et al., 2001). Put simply, a MANOVA and several ANOVAs each using the same measured outcome variables test completely different and irreconcilable effects, because the ANOVAs do not consider the relationships among the outcomes. These relationships are an essential consideration in the multivariate analyses, as illustrated in the Thompson (1999a) heuristic example.

In the words of Borgen and Seling (1978), "When data truly are multivariate, as implied by the application of MANOVA, a multivariate follow-up technique seems necessary to 'discover' the complexity of the data" (p. 696). It is illogical to first declare interest in a multivariate omnibus system of variables, and then to explore detected effects in this multivariate world by conducting nonmultivariate tests.

A logical MANOVA post hoc method is descriptive discriminant analysis, which Huberty (1994) noted is "closely aligned to the study of effects determined by a multivariate analysis of variance (MANOVA)" (p. 30). Huberty (1994) provided several chapters on using DDA post hoc to MANOVA to assess and describe multivariate dynamics.

Quality Indicators:

- Univariate methods are not used in the presence of multiple outcome variables.
- Univariate methods are not used post hoc to multivariate tests.

Failure to Test Statistical Assumptions

All statistical methods require that certain assumptions (e.g., homogeneity of variance in ANOVA, homogeneity of regression slopes in ANCOVA) must be met in order for p values and effect sizes to be accurate. Methodological assumptions are never perfectly met, but must be at least approximately met in order for results to be approximately correct.

Empirical studies of published articles suggest that statistical assumptions are too rarely tested by researchers (Keselman et al., 1998). These assumptions are more important than many researchers may realize, as suggested by Wilcox (1998) in his article titled, "How many discoveries have been lost by ignoring modern statistical methods?"

Statistical assumptions can be particularly important when statistical corrections are invoked, as in ANCOVA, particularly when used with nonrandom intact intervention groups (see Thompson, 1992). Using ANCOVA when the homogeneity of regression assumption is not met leads to "tragically misleading analyses" that actually "can mistakenly make compensatory education look harmful" (Campbell & Erlebacher, 1975, p. 597).

Quality Indicator:

- Persuasive evidence is explicitly presented that the assumptions of statistical methods are sufficiently well-met for results to be deemed credible.

Confidence Intervals for Reliability Coefficients, Statistics, and Effect Sizes

Confidence intervals (CIs) can be used to determine whether a given null hypothesis would be rejected. If a hypothesized value (e.g., $r = 0$; $r = .5$) is not within the interval, the null hypothesis positing the parameter value is rejected. However, this use of confidence intervals does not tap the primary positive features of using confidence intervals (Thompson, 1998a, 2001).

Confidence intervals inform judgment regarding all the values of the parameter that appear to be plausible, given the data (Cumming & Finch, 2001). Thus, by comparing the overlaps of confidence intervals across studies, researchers can evaluate the *consistency* of evidence across studies (Thompson, 2002b).

The widths of confidence intervals within a study, or across studies, also provide critical information regarding the *precision* of estimates in a study or in a literature. When intervals are wide, the evidence for a given point estimate being correct is called into question. Researchers may overinterpret effects in a literature and not recognize the imprecision of a body of literature, unless confidence intervals are computed and directly compared across studies.

For these various reasons, confidence intervals are increasingly recognized as being "in general, *the best* reporting strategy" and "the use of confidence intervals is therefore *strongly recommended*" (American Psychological Association, 2001, p. 22, emphasis added). Of course, as Fidler, Thomason, Cumming, Finch, and Leeman (2004) pointed out, as with any other statistical methods, CIs are not a panacea, and can be used thoughtlessly.

Univariate methods are generally inappropriate in the presence of multiple outcomes variables.

Common Mistakes

Some researchers misinterpret confidence intervals as telling us how confident we may be (e.g., 95%) that a given, single interval captures a population parameter, such as a correlational effect size (e.g., r, $r2$).

However, the confidence statements when dealing with confidence intervals are about a large or infinite set of intervals drawn from a population capturing the interval a given percentage (e.g., 95%) of the time, and these confidence statements are *not* about single intervals (Thompson, 2002b).

We never know, unless we have the population data (and then would not be computing a CI), whether our single interval does or does not capture a population parameter. The probabilities of intervals capturing the population parameter (e.g., r, $r2$) may be different even for a series of 95% confidence intervals.

Confidence intervals can be computed for (a) reliability coefficients (Fan & Thompson, 2001); (b) sample statistics (e.g., M, r); and (c) effect sizes (Thompson, 2002b). CIs are so appealing because using intervals across studies will ultimately lead us to the correct population value, even if our initial expectations are wildly in error (Schmidt, 1996)! Software for computing confidence intervals for effect sizes is widely available (Algina & Keselman, 2003; Cumming & Finch, 2001; Smithson, 2001; Steiger & Fouladi, 1992). Kline's (2004) recent book provides a comprehensive tutorial.

Quality Indicators:

- Confidence intervals are reported for the reliability coefficients derived for study data.
- Confidence intervals are reported for the sample statistics (e.g., means, correlation coefficients) of primary interest in the study.

- Confidence intervals are reported for study effect sizes.
- Confidence intervals are interpreted by direct and explicit comparison with related CIs from prior studies.

Summary

Within the quantitative group-design genre, only true experiments offer definitive evidence for causal inferences that can inform evidence-based instructional practice. But not all educational interventions are readily amenable to experiments. In addition, experimental studies of educational interventions are compromised by cross-contamination when students participate in multiple interventions.

In such cases correlational evidence may be useful in adducing complementary evidence. Correlational studies can produce intriguing results that are then subjected to experimental study. And correlational evidence can at least tentatively inform evidence-based practice when sophisticated causal modeling (e.g., regression discontinuity analyses) or exclusion methods are employed. Correlational evidence is most informative when exemplary practices are followed with regard to (a) measurement, (b) quantifying effects, (c) avoidance of common macro-analytic errors, and (d) use of confidence intervals to portray the *consistency* of possible effects and the *precisions* of the effect estimates. Table 1 presents a list of the quality indicators suggested for research in this genre.

Table 1. Suggested Quality Indicators for Correlational Research

Measurement	Practical and Clinical Significance	Avoiding Some Common Macro-Analytic Mistakes	CIs for Reliability Coefficients, Statistics, and Effect Sizes
1. Score reliability coefficients are reported for all measured variables, based on induction from a prior study or test manual, with explicit and reasonable justifications as regards comparabilities of (a) sample compositions and (b) score dispersions. 2. Score reliability coefficients are reported for all measured variables, based on analysis of the data in hand in the particular study. 3. Evidence is inducted, with explicit rationale, from a prior study or test manual that suggests scores are valid for the inferences being made in the study. 4. Score validity is empirically evaluated based on data generated within the study. 5. The influences of score reliability and validity on study interpretations are explicitly considered inreasonable detail.	6. One or more effect size statistics is reported for each study primary outcome, and the effect statistic used is clearly identified. 7. Authors interpret study effect sizes for selected practices by directly and explicitly comparing study effects with those reported in related prior studies. 8. Authors explicitly consider study design and effect size statistic limitations as part of effect interpretation.	9. GLM weights (e.g., beta weights) are interpreted as reflecting correlations of predictors with outcome variables only in the exceptional case that the weights indeed are correlation coefficients. 10. When noteworthy results are detected, and the origins of these effects are investigated, the interpretation includes examination of structure coefficients. 11. Interval data are not converted to nominal scale, unless such choices are justified on the extraordinary basis of distribution shapes, and the consequences of the conversion are thoughtfully considered as part of result interpretation. 12. Univariate methods are not used in the presence of multiple outcome variables. 13. Univariate methods are not used post hoc to multivariate tests. 14. Persuasive evidence is explicitly presented that the assumptions of statistical methods are sufficiently well-met for results to be deemed credible.	15. Confidence intervals are reported for the reliability coefficients derived for study data. 16. Confidence intervals are reported for the sample statistics (e.g., means, correlation coefficients) of primary interest in the study. 17. Confidence intervals are reported for study effect sizes. 18. Confidence intervals are interpreted by direct and explicit comparison with related CIs from prior studies.

References

Algina, J., & Keselman, H. J. (2003). Approximate confidence intervals for effect sizes. *Educational and Psychological Measurement, 63*, 537–553.

American Psychological Association. (2001). *Publication manual of the American Psychological Association* (5th ed.). Washington, DC: Author.

Anderson, D. R., Burnham, K. P., & Thompson, W. (2000). Null hypothesis testing: Problems, prevalence, and an alternative. *Journal of Wildlife Management, 64*, 912–923.

Atkinson, R. C., & Jackson, G. B. (Eds.). (1992). *Research and education reform: Roles for the Office of Educational Research and Improvement*. Washington, DC: National Academy of Sciences. (ERIC Document Reproduction Service No. ED 343 961)

Bagozzi, R. P. (1980). Performance and satisfaction in an industrial sales force: An examination of their antecedents and simultaneity. *Journal of Marketing, 44*, 65–77.

Bagozzi, R. P., Fornell, C., & Larcker, D. F. (1981). Canonical correlation analysis as a special case of a structural relations model. *Multivariate Behavioral Research, 16*, 437–454.

Berliner, D. C. (2002). Educational research: The hardest science of all. *Educational Researcher, 31*(8), 18–20.

Borgen, F. H., & Seling, M. J. (1978). Uses of discriminant analysis following MANOVA: Multivariate statistics for multivariate purposes. *Journal of Applied Psychology, 63*, 689–697.

Brennan, R. L. (2001). Some problems, pitfalls, and paradoxes in educational measurement. *Educational Measurement: Issues and Practices, 20*(4), 6–18.

Campbell, D. T., & Erlebacher, A. (1975). How regression artifacts in quasiexperimental evaluations can mistakenly make compensatory education look harmful. In M. Guttentag & E. L. Struening (Eds.), *Handbook of evaluation research* (Vol. 1, pp. 597–617). Beverly Hills, CA: Sage.

Chambless, D. (1998). Defining empirically supported therapies. *Journal of Consulting and Clinical Psychology, 66*, 7–18.

Chandler, R. (1957). The statistical concepts of confidence and significance. *Psychological Bulletin, 54*, 429–430.

Cliff, N. (1987). *Analyzing multivariate data*. San Diego, CA: Harcourt Brace Jovanovich.

Cohen, J. (1968). Multiple regression as a general dataanalytic system. *Psychological Bulletin, 70*, 426–443.

Cohen, J. (1994). The earth is round (*p* < .05). *American Psychologist, 49*, 997–1003.

Courville, T., & Thompson, B. (2001). Use of structure coefficients in published multiple regression articles: ß is not enough. *Educational and Psychological Measurement, 61*, 229–248.

Crocker, L., & Algina, J. (1986). *Introduction to classical and modern test theory*. New York: Holt, Rinehart & Winston.

Cumming, G., & Finch, S. (2001). A primer on the understanding, use and calculation of confidence intervals that are based on central and noncentral distributions. *Educational and Psychological Measurement, 61*, 532–575.

Duncan, O. D. (1975). *Introduction to structural equation models*. New York: Academic Press.

Dunlap, W. P., & Landis, R. S. (1998). Interpretations of multiple regression borrowed from factor analysis and canonical correlation. *The Journal of General Psychology, 125*, 397–407.

Fan, X., & Thompson, B. (2001). Confidence intervals about score reliability coefficients, please: An *EPM* guidelines editorial. *Educational and Psychological Measurement, 61*, 517–531.

Feuer, M. J., Towne, L., & Shavelson, R. J. (2002). Scientific culture and educational research. *Educational Researcher, 31*(8), 4–14.

Fidler, F. (2002). The fifth edition of the APA *Publication Manual*: Why its statistics recommendations are so controversial. *Educational and Psychological Measurement, 62*, 749–770.

Fidler, F., Thomason, N., Cumming, G., Finch, S. & Leeman, J. (2004). Editors can lead researchers to confidence intervals, but they can't make them think: Statistical reform lessons from medicine. *Psychological Science, 15*, 119–127.

Fish, L. J. (1988). Why multivariate methods are usually vital. *Measurement and Evaluation in Counseling and Development, 21*, 130–137.

Gall, M. D., Borg, W. R., & Gall, J. P. (1996). *Educational research: An introduction* (6th ed.). White Plains, NY: Longman.

Glass, G. V., McGaw, B., & Smith, M. L. (1981). *Meta-analysis in social research.* Beverly Hills, CA: Sage.

Gorsuch, R. L. (1983). *Factor analysis* (2nd ed.). Hillsdale, NJ: Erlbaum.

Graham, J. M., Guthrie, A. C., & Thompson, B. (2003). Consequences of not interpreting structure coefficients in published CFA research: A reminder. *Structural Equation Modeling, 10,* 142–153.

Harlow, L. L., Mulaik, S. A., & Steiger, J. H. (Eds.). (1997). *What if there were no significance tests?* Mahwah, NJ: Erlbaum.

Hester, Y. C. (2000). An analysis of the use and misuse of ANOVA. (Doctoral dissertation, Texas A&M University, 2000). *Dissertation Abstracts International, 61,* 4332A. (UMI No. 9994257)

Huberty, C. J. (1994). *Applied discriminant analysis.* New York: Wiley & Sons.

Huberty, C. J. (2002). A history of effect size indices. *Educational and Psychological Measurement, 62,* 227–240.

Jacobson, N. S., Roberts, L. J., Berns, S. B., & McGlinchey, J. B. (1999). Methods for defining and determining the clinical significance of treatment effects: Description, application, and alternatives. *Journal of Consulting and Clinical Psychology, 67,* 300–307.

Jöreskog, K. G. (1969). A general approach to confirmatory maximum likelihood factor analysis. *Psychometrika, 34,* 183-220.

Jöreskog, K. G. (1970). A general method for analysis of covariance structures. *Biometrika, 57,* 239–251.

Jöreskog, K. G. (1971). Simultaneous factor analysis in several populations. *Psychometrika, 36,* 409–426.

Jöreskog, K. G. (1978). Structural analysis of covariance and correlation matrices. *Psychometrika, 43,* 443–477.

Jöreskog, K. G., & Sörbom, D. (1989). *LISREL 7: A guide to the program and applications* (2nd ed.). Chicago: SPSS.

Kendall, P. C. (1999). Clinical significance. *Journal of Consulting and Clinical Psychology, 67,* 283–284.

Kerlinger, F. N. (1986). *Foundations of behavioral research* (3rd ed.). New York: Holt, Rinehart & Winston.

Keselman, H. J., Huberty, C. J, Lix, L. M., Olejnik, S., Cribbie, R., Donahue, B., et al. (1998). Statistical practices of educational researchers: An analysis of their ANOVA, MANOVA and ANCOVA analyses. *Review of Educational Research, 68,* 350–386.

Kieffer, K. M., Reese, R. J., & Thompson, B. (2001). Statistical techniques employed in *AERJ* and *JCP* articles from 1988 to 1997: A methodological review. *Journal of Experimental Education, 69,* 280–309.

Kirk, R. (1996). Practical significance: A concept whose time has come. *Educational and Psychological Measurement, 56,* 746–759.

Kline, R. (2004). *Beyond significance testing: Reforming data analysis methods in behavioral research.* Washington, DC: American Psychological Association.

Knapp, T. R. (1978). Canonical correlation analysis: A general parametric significance testing system. *Psychological Bulletin, 85,* 410–416.

Ludbrook, J., & Dudley, H. (1998). Why permutation tests are superior to *t* and *F* tests in medical research. *The American Statistician, 52,* 127–132.

McLean, J. E., & Kaufman, A. S. (2000). Editorial: Statistical significance testing and other changes to *Research in the Schools, 7*(2), 1–2.

Mosteller, F., & Boruch, R. (Eds.). (2002). *Evidence matters: Randomized trials in education research.* Washington, DC: Brookings Institution Press.

Nickerson, R. S. (2000). Null hypothesis significance testing: A review of an old and continuing controversy. *Psychological Methods, 5,* 241–301.

Olejnik, S., & Algina, J. (2000). Measures of effect size for comparative studies: Applications, interpretations, and limitations. *Contemporary Educational Psychology, 25,* 241–286.

Pedhazur, E. J. (1982). *Multiple regression in behavioral research: Explanation and prediction* (2nd ed.). New York: Holt, Rinehart & Winston.

Sackett, D. L., Straus, S. E., Richardson, W. S., Rosenberg, W., & Haynes, R. B. (2000). *Evidence-based medicine: How to practice and teach EBM* (2nd ed.). New York: Churchill Livingstone.

Schmidt, F. L. (1996). Statistical significance testing and cumulative knowledge in psychology: Implications for the training of researchers. *Psychological Methods, 1,* 115–129.

Schmidt, F. L., & Hunter, J. E. (1977). Development of a general solution to the problem of validity generalization. *Journal of Applied Psychology, 62*, 529–540.

Shavelson, R. J., & Towne, L. (Eds.). (2002). *Scientific research in education*. Washington, DC: National Academy Press.

Smithson, M. (2001). Correct confidence intervals for various regression effect sizes and parameters: The importance of noncentral distributions in computing intervals. *Educational and Psychological Measurement, 61*, 605–632.

Snyder, P. (1991). Three reasons why stepwise regression methods should not be used by researchers. In B. Thompson (Ed.), *Advances in educational research: Substantive findings, methodological developments* (Vol. 1, pp. 99–105). Greenwich, CT: JAI Press.

Snyder, P. (2000). Guidelines for reporting results of group quantitative investigations. *Journal of Early Intervention, 23*, 145–150.

Snyder, P., & Lawson, S. (1993). Evaluating results using corrected and uncorrected effect size estimates. *Journal of Experimental Education, 61*, 334–349.

Spearman, C. (1904). The proof and measurement of association between two things. *Journal of Psychology, 15*, 72–101.

Steiger, J. H., & Fouladi, R. T. (1992). *R*2: A computer program for interval estimation, power calculation, and hypothesis testing for the squared multiple correlation. *Behavior Research Methods, Instruments, and Computers, 4*, 581–582.

Thompson, B. (1984). *Canonical correlation analysis: Uses and interpretation*. Newbury Park, CA: Sage.

Thompson, B. (1986). ANOVA versus regression analysis of ATI designs: An empirical investigation. *Educational and Psychological Measurement, 46*, 917–928.

Thompson, B. (1992). Misuse of ANCOVA and related "statistical control" procedures. *Reading Psychology, 13*, iii–xviii.

Thompson, B. (1995). Stepwise regression and stepwise discriminant analysis need not apply here: A guidelines editorial. *Educational and Psychological Measurement, 55*, 525–534.

Thompson, B. (1996). AERA editorial policies regarding statistical significance testing: Three suggested reforms. *Educational Researcher, 25*(2), 26–30.

Thompson, B. (1998a). In praise of brilliance: Where that praise really belongs. *American Psychologist, 53*, 799–800.

Thompson, B. (1998b, July). *The ten commandments of good Structural Equation Modeling behavior: A userfriendly, introductory primer on SEM.* Paper presented at the annual meeting of the U.S. Department of Education, Office of Special Education Programs Project Directors' Conference, Washington, DC. (ERIC Document Reproduction Service No. ED 420 154)

Thompson, B. (1999a, April). *Common methodology mistakes in educational research, revisited, along with a primer on both effect sizes and the bootstrap.* Paper presented at the annual meeting of the American Educational Research Association, Montreal, Canada. (ERIC Document Reproduction Service No. ED 429 110)

Thompson, B. (1999b). Improving research clarity and usefulness with effect size indices as supplements to statistical significance tests. *Exceptional Children, 65*, 329–337.

Thompson, B. (2000a). Canonical correlation analysis. In L. Grimm & P. Yarnold (Eds.), *Reading and understanding more multivariate statistics* (pp. 285–316). Washington, DC: American Psychological Association.

Thompson, B. (2000b). Ten commandments of structural equation modeling. In L. Grimm & P. Yarnold (Eds.), *Reading and understanding more multivariate statistics* (pp. 261–284). Washington, DC: American Psychological Association.

Thompson, B. (2001). Significance, effect sizes, stepwise methods, and other issues: Strong arguments move the field. *Journal of Experimental Education, 70*, 80–93.

Thompson, B. (2002a). "Statistical," "practical," and "clinical": How many kinds of significance do counselors need to consider? *Journal of Counseling and Development, 80*, 64–71.

Thompson, B. (2002b). What future quantitative social science research could look like: Confidence intervals for effect sizes. *Educational Researcher, 31*(3), 24–31.

Thompson, B. (Ed.). (2003). *Score reliability: Contemporary thinking on reliability issues.* Newbury Park, CA: Sage.

Thompson, B. (in press-a). Research synthesis: Effect sizes. In G. Camilli, P. B. Elmore, & J. Green (Eds.), *Complementary methods for research in education*. Washington, DC: American Educational Research Association.

Thompson, B. (in press-b). The "significance" crisis in psychology and education. *Journal of Socio-Economics*.

Thompson, B., & Borrello, G. M. (1985). The importance of structure coefficients in regression research. *Educational and Psychological Measurement, 45*, 203–209.

Vacha-Haase, T. (1998). Reliability generalization: Exploring variance in measurement error affecting score reliability across studies. *Educational and Psychological Measurement, 58*, 6–20.

Vacha-Haase, T., Henson, R. K., & Caruso, J. (2002). Reliability generalization: Moving toward improved understanding and use of score reliability. *Educational and Psychological Measurement, 62*, 562–569.

Vacha-Haase, T., Kogan, L. R., & Thompson, B. (2000). Sample compositions and variabilities in published studies versus those in test manuals: Validity of score reliability inductions. *Educational and Psychological Measurement, 60*, 509–522.

Vacha-Haase, T., Nilsson, J. E., Reetz, D. R., Lance, T. S., & Thompson, B. (2000). Reporting practices and APA editorial policies regarding statistical significance and effect size. *Theory & Psychology, 10*, 413–425. Whittington, D. (1998). How well do researchers report their measures? An evaluation of measurement in published educational research. *Educational and Psychological Measurement, 58*, 21–37.

Wilcox, R. R. (1998). How many discoveries have been lost by ignoring modern statistical methods? *American Psychologist, 53*, 300–314.

Wilkinson, L., & APA Task Force on Statistical Inference. (1999). Statistical methods in psychology journals: Guidelines and explanations. *American Psychologist, 54*, 594–604. [reprint available through the APA Home Page: http://www.apa.org/journals/amp/amp548594.html]

Wright, S. (1921). Correlation and causality. *Journal of Agricultural Research, 20*, 557–585.

Wright, S. (1934). The method of path coefficients. *Annals of Mathematical Statistics, 5*, 161–215

About the Authors

Bruce Thompsom (CEC TX Federation), Texas A & M University and Baylor College of Medicine, College Station, Texas.

Karen E. Diamond (CEC IN Federation), Professor and Director, Child Development Laboratory School, Purdue University, W. Lafayette, Indiana.

Robin McWilliam, Director, Center for Child Development, Professor of Pediatrics and Special Education, Vanderbilt University Medical Center, Nashville, Tennessee.

Patricia Snyder (CEC #514), Associate Dean for Research and Graduate Studies, Louisiana State University Health Science Center, New Orleans.

Scott W. Snyder (CEC #144), School of Education Dean's Office, University of Alabama, Birmingham.

Correspondence concerning this article should be addressed to Bruce Thompson, TAMU Department of Educational Psychology, Texas A&M University, College Station, TX 77843-4225, or via e-mail using the Internet URL: http://www.coe.tamu.edu/-bthompson.

Appendix C

Where to Find Evidence-Based Interventions

(Excerpted from *Identifying and Implementing Educational Practices Supported by Rigorous Evidence: A User Friendly Guide*, U.S. Department of Education, Institute of Education Sciences)

The following web sites can be useful in finding evidence-based educational interventions. These sites use varying criteria for determining which interventions are supported by evidence, but all distinguish between randomized controlled trials and other types of supporting evidence. We recommend that, in navigating these web sites, you use this guide to help you make independent judgments about whether the listed interventions are supported by "strong" evidence, "possible" evidence, or neither.

The What Works Clearinghouse

(http://www.w-w-c.org/) established by the U.S. Department of Education's Institute of Education Sciences to provide educators, policymakers, and the public with a central, independent, and trusted source of scientific evidence of what works in education.

The Promising Practices Network

(http://www.promisingpractices.net/) web site highlights programs and practices that credible research indicates are effective in improving outcomes for children, youth, and families.

Blueprints for Violence Prevention

(http://www.colorado.edu/cspv/blueprints/index.html) is a national violence prevention initiative to identify programs that are effective in reducing adolescent violent crime, aggression, delinquency, and substance abuse.

The International Campbell Collaboration

(http://www.campbellcollaboration.org/Fralibrary.html) offers a registry of systematic reviews of evidence on the effects of interventions in the social, behavioral, and educational arenas.

Social Programs That Work

(http://www.excelgov.org/displayContent.asp?Keyword=prppcSocial) offers a series of papers developed by the Coalition for Evidence-Based Policy on social programs that are backed by rigorous evidence of effectiveness.

ORDER FORM FOR RELATED RESOURCES

E R S

Quantity	Item Number	Title	Base Price	ERS Individual Subscriber Discount Price	ERS School District Subscriber Discount Price	Total Price
				Price per Item		
	0713	*Implementing the Findings of Research: Bridging the Gap Between Knowledge and Practice*	$28	$21	$14	
	0538	*Handbook of Research on Improving Student Achievement, Third Edition*	$44	$33	$22	
	0738	*Data-Based Decision Making, Second Edition*	$26.95	$19.95	$19.95	
	0496	*Understanding and Using Education Statistics: It's Easier (and More Important) Than You Think, Second Edition*	$20	$15	$10	
		Shipping and Handling** (Add the greater of $4.50 or 10% of purchase price.)				
		Express Delivery** (Add $20 for second-business-day service.)				
	**Please double for international orders.				TOTAL PRICE:	

SATISFACTION GUARANTEED! If you are not satisfied with an ERS resource, return it in its original condition within 30 days of receipt and we will give you a full refund.

Visit us online at www.ers.org for a complete listing of resources!

Method of payment:

☐ Check enclosed (payable to ERS)   ☐ P.O. enclosed (Purchase order #_____)

☐ MasterCard   ☐ VISA   ☐ American Express

Name on Card: _____   Credit Card #:_____

Expiration Date: _____   Signature: _____

Ship to: (please print or type)   ☐ Dr.   ☐ Mr.   ☐ Mrs.   ☐ Ms.

Name: _____   Position: _____

School District or Agency: _____   ERS Subscriber ID#: _____

Street Address: _____

City, State, Zip: _____

Telephone: _____   Fax: _____

Email: _____

Return completed order form to:
Educational Research Service • 1001 North Fairfax Street, Suite 500 • Alexandria, VA 22314-1587
Phone: 703-243-2100 • Toll Free Phone: 800-791-9308 • Fax: 703-243-1985 • Toll Free Fax: 800-791-9309
Email: ers@ers.org • Web site: www.ers.org

ERS Subscriptions at a Glance

If you are looking for reliable preK-12 research to . . .

- tackle the challenges of NCLB;

- identify research-based teaching practices;

- make educationally sound and cost-effective decisions; and most importantly

- improve student achievement . . .

then look no further than an ERS Subscription.

Simply pick the subscription option that best meets your needs:

■ **School District Subscription**—a special research and information subscription that provides education leaders with timely research on priority issues in preK-12 education. All new ERS publications and periodicals, access to customized information services through the ERS special library, and 50 percent discounts on additional ERS resources are included in this subscription for one annual fee. This subscription also provides the entire administrative staff "instant" online, searchable access to the wide variety of ERS resources. You'll gain access to the ERS electronic library of more than 1,600 educational research-based documents, as well as additional content uploaded throughout the year.

■ **Individual Subscription**—designed primarily for school administrators, staff, and school board members who want to receive a personal copy of new ERS studies, reports, and/or periodicals published and special discounts on other resources purchased.

■ **Other Education Agency Subscription**—available for state associations, libraries, departments of education, service centers, and other organizations needing access to quality research and information resources and services.

Your ERS Subscription benefits begin as soon as your order is received and continue for 12 months. For more detailed subscription information and pricing, contact ERS toll free at 800-791-9308, by email at ers@ers.org, or visit us online at www.ers.org!